THE TRACTION ENGINE ARCHIVE

Volume 3

The Transitional Years

By

John H. Meredith

EDDISON
9699

THE TRACTION ENGINE ARCHIVE

Volume 3

The Transitional Years

By

John H. Meredith

Registered Charity No. 1102574

Published by The Road Locomotive Society
PO Box 1878, Andover SP10 9AU

ISBN 978-0-9508480-4-4

Page Layout and Printed by The Amadeus Press, Cleckheaton, West Yorkshire.

FOREWORD

Having written the first two volumes of The Traction Engine Archive, I was delighted when John Meredith, who is preparing this third volume, asked me to write the foreword. This work concentrates on a later period than in the earlier books and most of the photographs are from John's own camera. Many are from the last days of working road steam when some of the subjects were well past their heyday and getting worn and tired. Other engines were still kept in excellent condition, particularly some of the local authority owned rollers. Disused engines are also seen, often standing forlorn and derelict. Then with its modest beginnings we see the start of the preservation era, given initial publicity by Arthur Napper's activities at Appleford which were well reported in the press at the time. Who could ever have realised it would result in the huge movement we have today with engines returning from all corners of the globe, restoration of total wrecks, and the high prices they now fetch? This work mainly covers the earlier years of preservation when most engines were seen much as they finished their work but there is a synopsis of later events to bring the record up to the present time.

The book covers an important period in the history of our well loved engines which has been rather overlooked. Although I am younger than John, it is a period I can relate to, having bought my first engine in 1954 whilst still at school and when much of the other machinery appearing at today's "traction engine rallies" had not then even been made. The modest price, by present day standards, of £50 for my first engine took a lot of finding, with no parental help or encouragement. At this time there were still plenty of men about who had worked with steam, either as owners or employees, and although nearly extinct on the roads, steam traction still thrived on the railways, and indeed new main line steam engines were built up to 1960. I always found much help and encouragement from the people involved, and I learnt a lot, not only about the practical side but also about local engine history. I owe them a debt of gratitude for their friendship, the passing on of knowledge and in some cases, their considerable practical help. Most of these people who at one time earned a living with steam are now gone and we in the engine movement are the poorer for their passing.

Perhaps now a few recollections of my own might not come amiss. As the book tends to concentrate on the Southeast, other areas, such as my home area of Gloucestershire, are less well covered. Here the County Council still had a fleet of well maintained steam rollers, mostly Avelings, some bought new, others from the government after World War I, and still others taken over from local rural district councils. The latter group included all the non-Avelings. Contractors rollers were also seen at work or in transit between jobs, and always seemed to be Avelings. These were owned by firms such as Bomford & Evershed, Buncombe, R.C. Moore of Gloucester, A.C. Canton of Sheepscome and one or two others. A very grimy Sentinel, owned by Llewellyns of Ross-on-Wye, made fairly frequent visits to Stroud Gas Works to collect tar, whilst Glossops Sentinels were regular summer visitors on tarring and gritting work. They parked up at the Stoudwater Canal Wharf some half a mile from where I am writing these notes. Two very late S4 Sentinels operated out of the Chipping Sodbury area, one owned by Virgo, the other by Washbourne, the pair lasting until nationalisation of the road transport industry. I have always regretted not seeing a working showman's engine — the last recorded in the area was a Fowler in 1944. I was then 7 so I feel I should have seen it. That was also the year when Jesse Vines finished with steam for threshing, another activity I am sorry to have missed, although both these happenings persisted longer elsewhere. The only traction engine, I ever saw in real work was the 6 nhp Marshall at the Ide Sawmill near Exeter which continued until the early nineteen-sixties. Further afield I saw a Ransomes portable competently driving a country sawmill in France as late as 1977. Well, enough of my memories, tour the pages and enjoy what John has to show you.

Richard Willcox
Chairman, Road Locomotive Society

CONTENTS

ACKNOWLEDGEMENTS

My interest in road steam was kindled by chance meetings with Derek Stoyel and Philip Bradley who, as I found out later, were both prominent members of the Road Locomotive Society. This led me to join the Society and then to meet many other members, both professional and amateur, who had great knowledge of the subject and I was encouraged to extend my interest in photography to record the contemporary scene. Even so my opportunities were limited and I am most grateful to the following friends who have enabled me to fill some gaps:

Ken Bargh	Photo 77		Harry Luff	Photo	26, 32
Ted Crawforth	Photo	cover, 41	Bob Pratt	Photo	112
Ian Davidson	Photo	97	Don Thompson	Photo	8, 47, 85, 88
Bill Haynes	Photo	78			95, 105, 106
Keith Langston	Photo	206	Richard Willcox	Photo	199
Rev Norman Lemprière	Photo	92	Peter Williams	Photo	18, 19, 87
			Jack Wyse	Photo	73

In drafting the narrative I have had assistance from Tony Coombes, Robin Harding, Bill Love, Derek Rayner, Bob Schofield, Frank Strange and, in particular, from Peter Smart who has answered many queries and worked wonders in preparing electronic copy for the printers. I thank all of these together with the Society's enthusiastic Chairman, Richard Willcox, for his encouragement and for writing the Foreword. Two names from the past have truly made their mark on the contents – John L. Smith (Lens of Sutton) who had his ear firmly to the ground and directed me to many photographic opportunities and Alan Duke, the Society Records Officer, for his painstaking compilation of engine records which have given an added dimension to many of the captions. The final photograph (No. 208) is in tribute to him.

FRONT COVER ILLUSTRATION

The most prestigious event in today's traction engine calendar is the Great Dorset Steam Fair when over two hundred engines take part along with a vast array of supporting attractions. Some of the most stirring sights are in heavy haulage as engines pound up the steep gradients. In this scene from the 2004 Fair the leading engine is Geoff & Veronica Mathews' Fowler No.11111 of 1910, registered BE 7988, followed by Graham Love's Fowler No.15323 of 1918 and registered HR 3697. Perched on the trailer is Tasker traction engine No.1709 which is also featured in photo 192. (TED CRAWFORTH)

FRONTISPIECE

1. A commonplace scene in the immediate postwar period. Parked up for the weekend on a building site in Mitcham, South London, is Eddison roller No.423. This is Aveling & Porter piston valve single cylinder roller No.10422 of 1922 and registered FX 9699. Note the driver's living van, just visible behind the roller. The photograph was taken on Sunday, 18th September 1949.

The Transitional Years

Introduction

When the Road Locomotive Society was formed in 1937, steam road engines were still in widespread use and examples were still being built. Aveling-Barford continued building steam rollers until 1948, Sentinel built 100 waggons for the Argentine in 1950/51, Marshalls built several rollers during World War II and then went on to supply boilers and other parts for India in 1961/62 whilst Fosters sold the last traction engine for commercial use in this country in 1944 (No.14738). In 1948 several ploughing engines were overhauled and sent to work on the ground-nuts scheme in Tanganyika (Tanzania). However, the outlook for road steam vehicles was bleak and although wartime shortages had extended the working lives of many engines, scrap drives had resulted in countless others going to the breakers. In the immediate post-war period the decline in numbers increased rapidly, spurred on by sales of vehicles from the services and changes in agricultural methods.

Steam rollers were least affected and were in extensive use until the mid-fifties. Other types became increasingly rare, none more so than traction engines and road locomotives. On the fairground, most steam driven roundabouts were electrified but one type of ride remained faithful to steam power, the giant swing yachts. Some steam wagons remained as load carriers and an appreciable number survived as tar sprayers and road planers where they escaped the pernicious taxation bestowed on steam haulage vehicles. To round off the commercial scene, a few engines devoted to special purposes continued in use; some of these are featured on these pages, such as the Sentinels at Teignmouth Quay, Fodens at Croydon and Portsmouth and ploughing engines on dredging work.

With such poor prospects for the survival of steam power on the roads, the Road Locomotive Society did what it could to encourage preservation. Luckily, there were a few users of engines so interested; first and foremost was Chris Lambert of Horsmonden, Kent, another was W.J. Bishop of Northampton. Both of these benefactors presented engines to the Society which were intended to form the nucleus of a Museum; it was then thought that the best way of saving engines was to persuade an established Museum to take them. This was done successfully in the case of the historic Aveling & Porter traction engine (No.721 of 1871) which had been discovered in a very derelict condition. It was acquired by the Society, Aveling-Barford undertook its restoration and in 1953 it was presented to the Science Museum in South Kensington where it is on permanent display and kept in optimum conditions. An alternative idea was the establishment of the Society's own traction engine museum. This idea was actively pursued for some time but the major hurdle of land acquisition could not be accomplished and the three engines in the Society's ownership were reluctantly sold. Regrettably, two traction engines were scrapped (Burrell No. 1007 of 1883 and Ransomes No. 12456 of 1899) but the third engine, a tractor (Tasker No. 1666 of 1917), remains in preservation.

At this period the effect of greater leisure and wealth among the population was leading to all manner of pursuits being adopted and the owning of traction engines was one of these. Unlike railway locomotives, they do not need a track to run on and it was quite feasible for individuals to own and operate road locomotives, particularly if they came from rural areas with land and some workshop facilities available. The final inducement owners needed was to have somewhere to take their charges and this need was solved by the timely challenges made by Arthur Napper of Appleford to his engine owning friends. The races at Appleford on 30th July 1950 and at Nettlebed on 24th June 1951, achieved wide coverage in the national press and, with a lot of hard work on his part and some near financial disasters, his highly entertaining antics led the way to the development of traction engine rallies.

Arthur Napper's activities also led directly to the formation of the National Traction Engine Club in 1954 (now the National Traction Engine Trust). Once the new body had become established it quickly developed the preservation and rallying aspects of the movement and since then the Road Locomotive Society has concentrated on historical research and in particular the recording of engines and their manufacturers and users. Local clubs devoted to rallying have also been set up and nationally the Road Roller Association, the Steam Plough Club and bodies devoted to particular manufacturers have been formed. This has led to a proliferation of rallies and their popularity with the general public continues to this day, although they now feature all manner of other attractions besides steam engines. Many of the engines present at today's rallies could have been secured for a few pounds each in the nineteen-fifties but now change hands for six figure sums. It is a far cry from the solitary roller or steam wagon eking out its final years of commercial activity to the two hundred and fifty or so engines entertaining visitors at the annual Great Dorset Steam Fairs in the early years of the twenty-first century – a massive transition indeed.

List of Engines Depicted — (Photograph numbers are in italics)

ALLCHIN	*1105 – 168 *1131- 18 *1173 – 93 *3251 - 118
ALLEN	*67 - 127
ARMSTRONG WHITWORTH	*10R2 -169 10R32 - 19
ATKINSON	*72 – 198
AVELING BARFORD	*AC621 - 170
AVELING & PORTER	*721 – 120, 121 *1760 – 126 *2185 – 2 *3387 – 135 3799 – 114 4371 – 102 *4463 – 3 *4561 – 115 4988 – 14 5021 – 10 *6158 – 100 *6407 – 152
	7445 – 108 7828 – 12,13 *7838 – 206 *8036 – 16 8923 – 130 8985 – 4 *9010 – 114 9095 – 202 *9102 - 8 *9449 – 99 *10114 – 43,44 *10317 – 42
	10422 – 1 *10437 – 171 10792 – 37,38 10897 – 11 10998 – 7 11671 – 15 *12156 – 6 *12186 – 92 12621 – 5 *14008 – 9 *14068 – 200,201
BABCOCK & WILCOX	*95/4011 – 175
BROWN & MAY	*8742 – 172
BURRELL	*2003 – 173 *2421 – 154 2683 – 39 *2701 – 146,147 *2879 – 142,143 *2894 – 46 *3112 – 158 *3343 – 125 *3356 – 63 3364 – 20
	*3489 – 150 3799 – 114 *3804 – 146 *3865 – 49 *3884 – 45 *3912 – 124 *3949 – 48 3967 – 47 3988/4022 – 21 *4072 – 117
CLAYTON & SHUTTLEWORTH	*36336 – 119 *44103 – 134 *46823 – 174
DAVEY PAXMAN	*13073 – 176 *19413 – 118
FODEN	*4258 – 177 *5218 – 141 5788 – 74 *8304 – 75,76 *11340 – 177 *13008 – 86 13152 – 98 *13156 – 85 *13196 – 69
	*13358 - 137 *14078 – 137
FOSTER	12504 – 146 *12539 – 140 *14405/14446 – 50 14509 – 91 *14589 – 178 *14632 – 156,196
FOWELL	*98 – 179
FOWLER	7943 – 17 *9924 – 180 10958 – 22 *11111 – cover 11822 – 132 *12906 – 199 *13481/2 – 109 14047 – 107 14350 – 111 *14695 – 110
	*14862 – 197 *15323 – cover *15341 – 162 *15362 – 105,106 *15589 – 161 *15657 – 133 *20223 – 151 *21698 – 23
FYSON	T17 – 113
GARRETT	*27946 – 181 30159 – 153 32860 – 112 *33295 – 208 *33987 – 157 34181 – 98
GREEN	*1968 – 182
HORNSBY	*6557 - 189
MANN	*1145 – 183
MARSHALL	6402 – 101 *15391 – 136 *32092 – 184 *37690 – 128, 129, 130 *49725 – 160 *69326 – 130, 131 *73900 – 36 76555 – 29 *78724 – 24
	80730 – 26 85105 – 25 *87003 – 184 *87635 - 27
McLAREN	*1038 – 185 *1623 – 49 *1713 – 94
RANSOMES SIMS & JEFFERIES	*26995 – 186 *31066 – 138
ROBEY	*29330 – 187 *33957/40798 – 155 40798 – 155 41589-28 43886 – 66
RUSTON PROCTOR	*48359 – 188 52337 – 97
RUSTON & HORNSBY	52797 – 30 *115023 – 35 *169166 – 190
SAVAGE #	*421 – 55 *699 – 52 *704 – 54 *740 – 59 *867 – 60 886 – 61 901 – 64,65 ? – 53,62,67
SENTINEL	*1286 – 191 *1465 – 165 *2307 – 141 *2973 – 77 *5644 – 95 6258 – 72 6400 – 83 6606 – 88 7060 – 104 *7701 – 103 7888 – 79
	8385 – 84 *8454 – 89,90 *8562 – 71 *8590 – 204 8681 – 81,82 *8850 – 96 *8992 – 166 *9023 – 70 9227 - 68
TASKER	*1318 – 114,116 *1709 – cover, 192
THORNYCROFT	*39 – 148,149
WALKER	56
WALLIS & STEEVENS	*2149 – 207 *2694 – 193 7128 – 33 *7449 – 41 *7498 – 139 *7683 – 129,130 *7774 – 159 7785 – 32 7837 – 31 *8023 – 34
WANTAGE	*1376 – 194 *1389 – 144,145
YORKSHIRE	*940 – 195 1511 – 78 2189 – 87 2271 – 73
MISCELLANEOUS	40, 203, *205

Only ride engines are listed, not organ engines. * Engines still in existence (2008).

STEAM ROLLING

2. Most local authorities used steam rollers but no other machine, at least in the London area, was as old as Croydon Corporation's SR 600.This 15 ton single cylinder roller had been built by Aveling & Porter in1886, numbered 2185, and was maintained in excellent condition. It is working in London Road, Norbury, on 2nd July 1952, within 100 yards of my home. When steam rollers were required to be registered in 1921 the Croydon Borough Council appropriately allocated it "BY 2185" and then used the ensuing numbers for the other members of their fleet. The roller is now preserved by the Department of Science & Industry but it is not at the South Kensington Science Museum; it is relegated to their store at Wroughton near Swindon.

3. A few weeks earlier, on 14th May 1952 and on the same road, is Croydon's SR 602. This is Aveling & Porter 12 ½ ton overhead valve compound No.4463 built in 1899 and registered BY 2196. This roller was later sold to Hardwicks of Ewell but was resold into preservation.

4. Croydon's SR 603 was an Aveling & Porter 9 ton tandem roller with compound cylinders. A relative youngster in the fleet, it had been built in 1919, works No.8985, and registered BY 2199. It is seen in the Corporation's Factory Lane Depot on 22nd March 1951 and was reported as broken up in 1954.

5. Adjoining Croydon's southern boundary was Coulsdon & Purley UDC and they operated this small Aveling & Porter tandem roller, but it was out of use when I photographed it in the Council's Royal Oak Depot on 27th January 1951. It is one of the sophisticated 'O' type machines with twin high pressure cylinders, quick reverse and power steering. It had been built in 1930, No.12621, and registered PL 2747. (See also photographs 37 & 38.)

6. To the north of Croydon lay the megalopolis presided over by the London County Council. However, the LCC did not maintain the roads, this was the responsibility of the individual London Boroughs, and adjoining Croydon was the Borough of Wandsworth. Here we see that Council's No. 6, Aveling & Porter No.12156, new in 1928 and registered YW 4437. This is an 'F' type piston valve compound 10 ton roller and is seen returning to depot, crossing Bedford Hill railway bridge between Tooting and Streatham, on 22nd September 1951. Note the driver's bicycle slung behind the canopy, also the traditional Austin London Taxicab.

7. Further north still came the Borough of Lambeth and their roller is seen on the Vauxhall Cross gyratory road on 11th October 1952. It is an Aveling & Porter 'B' type piston valve compound 6 ton machine No.10998, registered XU 4081, and was built in 1924.

8. Roads in more rural areas were the responsibility of the County Councils and a very well turned out Essex County Council roller is seen at work on 27th June 1950. This is Aveling & Porter 10 ton slide valve single cylinder roller No.9102, new in 1920, and registered NO 1226. It carries the name "MARIA" on the front of the awning.
(DON THOMPSON)

9. Further into East Anglia, the City of Norwich operated this Aveling & Porter 10 ton slide valve compound roller, No.14008 of 1929 and registered VG 2269. It was numbered 7 in the municipal fleet and is seen working on one of the City's most well known thoroughfares, Carrow Road, on 28th June 1956.

10. Crossing from Norfolk in the east to Wales in the west, Holyhead UDC operated this Aveling & Porter 10 ton overhead valve compound roller No.5021 of 1902. There is no sign of a registration number on the engine or in the Road Locomotive Society records. It may have escaped licensing altogether! The photograph was taken on the opposite side of Anglesey to Holyhead, at Menai Bridge, on 4th July 1950.

11. The railway authorities were responsible for many miles of roadway at passenger and goods stations and where public roads crossed over railways. Much of the maintenance work was put out to contract but some was done in-house. The 'railway-owned' roller seen here is Aveling & Porter 'E' type piston valve single cylinder roller No.10897, registered TT 231, and built in 1924. It is working at New Wandsworth coal yard near Clapham Junction on 11th July 1951. The roller was numbered S 132 by British Railways, Southern Region, and worked at many locations in South and Southeast London. Its early history is uncertain but is thought to have been owned originally by Devon County Council and based at their Newton Abbot Depot before passing into railway ownership.

12. The largest rolling contractor in Britain was Eddison Plant Ltd of Dorchester and, with one of their depots at Kingston upon Thames, their rollers could be seen throughout the London area. In this scene Eddison No.199 is working on the widening of the approach road at Waterloo Station on 9th February 1951. With the 1951 Festival of Britain South Bank Exhibition being developed just across the road, the railway authorities were carrying out work to cater for the anticipated extra traffic that the Festival would bring.

13. No.199 again, but this time travelling between jobs with its living van and water cart in tow, with the driver eking out a spartan existence 'on the job'. No. 199 was Aveling & Porter 'BT' type roller No.7828, new to Eddison in 1912 and registered FX 7006. It spent all its working life with the firm and was sold for scrap in 1956. The photograph was taken in London Road, Norbury, on Saturday morning, 20th October 1951.

14. Rollers belonging to smaller contractors were also widespread and one firm who undertook much work in the London area was Rowley Plant Hire Co Ltd. Many such firms acquired their rollers second-hand and this one started its life as Eddison's No.111 in 1902. It later belonged to Friern Barnet UDC and went on to Rowleys in about 1929 where it became their fleet No. 6. It is an Aveling & Porter 10 ton single cylinder slide valve roller No.4988, registered FX 6938, and is seen outside the firm's Mitcham Depot on 1st October 1950.

15. Another Rowley Aveling & Porter but this time at a prestigious location – Horse Guards Parade – on 15th April 1954. This is a 'C' type 8 ton single cylinder piston valve machine, No.11671, and registered PF 5351. It is scarifying the parade ground some two months before the Trooping the Colour ceremony. Numbered 19 in the Rowley Plant fleet, it was new in 1926 to G.S. Faulkner & Son of Reigate and came to Rowleys after World War II.

16. Another contractor owned roller: A.J. Ward & Sons of Egham were using this slide valve compound Aveling & Porter on a housing development off the Wandsworth Road at Vauxhall on 16th August 1950. Works No.8036 and registered XN 4688, it was new to the Royal Borough of Kensington in 1913. There were two separate firms of Wards at Egham owned by brothers Alfred and Herbert. (See also photo 33.)

17. Over half the steam rollers used in Britain were built by Aveling & Porter but there were around a dozen other prominent manufacturers. Seen here is Fowler Class D2 12 ton single cylinder roller No.7943 built in 1899 and registered E 5356. It had belonged to the amalgamated firm of John Allen & Sons (Oxford) Ltd and Ford & Son (Wokingham) Ltd, with the former's name carried on a plate fixed to the headstock and the latter's plate carried on the motion cover. However, by the time this photograph was taken on the Oxford bypass on the 4th September 1955, the joint owners had been taken over by Eddison Plant Ltd. The original owner was McLoughlin & Robinson of Stoke-on-Trent so the 'E' (Staffordshire) registration was appropriate. The later change to 'EE' (Grimsby), as it appears here, is inexplicable.

18. Looking after their local industry, the County Borough of Northampton operated a pair of Allchin rollers. This is Borough Highways Department No.1, works No.1131, a 10 ton single cylinder roller built in 1900 and registered NH 3416. It is in the Corporation's Depot at St. James on 14th July 1951. This was the first of just a handful of rollers built by Wm. Allchin Ltd (PETER WILLIAMS)

19. The Manchester firm of Armstrong Whitworth produced steam rollers among various peacetime products following the reduction in armament requirements after the cessation of World War I. This is their No.10R32, built in 1925 and registered NE 2499, a 10 ton compound roller with piston valves. It was operated by William Prestwich. (PETER WILLIAMS)

20. Burrell Rollers were not so numerous as their traction engines but they could be found in most parts of the country. This is No.3364, a 10 ton double crank compound built in 1912 and registered MB 44. It was first operated by the Wirral District Council but was later absorbed into the Cheshire County Council fleet and as No. 20 is at their Hooton Depot on 3rd November 1951.

21. A more recent Burrell, this roller was built at Thetford in 1925 and was still with its original owner, J. Hardy of Blackmore, Essex, but when photographed on 13th January 1952 it was on the other side of the Thames at Northfleet in Kent. It is another double crank compound No.4022, registered PU 7453 and carries the name "LORNA". When built this engine was allocated No.3988 but the number was changed to 4022 before its sale to J. Hardy and is the number it always carried.

22. Fowler rollers were quite widespread and this Class D2 10 ton overhead valve compound is No.10958 built in 1907 and registered NY 2227. It is taking water at Hercules Road, Lambeth, on 3rd August 1950. At that time it was owned by Percy Parsons of Cheam, Surrey: the fleet number 26 on the headstock related to previous owner W.G. Smoothy, Rochford, Essex. Its first owner was in South Wales, hence its Glamorgan 'NY' registration.

23. Another Fowler but 30 years younger, Merioneth County Council No. 2, a Class DNA 12 ton compound dating from 1937. It is works No.21698, registered FF 4910 and is seen neatly parked up between Fairbourne and Arthog on 30th June 1964. This roller continued to serve Merioneth for several more years and is now preserved.

24. Another maker whose rollers were frequently seen was Marshalls of Gainsborough. Belonging to Rowley Plant Hire and under repair at their Mitcham Depot on 2nd December 1950 is No.78724, a 6 ton piston valve single cylinder roller built in 1925 and registered OPC 765. It originally carried registration MR 3101 but was requisitioned by the War Department during World War II and took its new registration after 'demob' in 1949.

25. A similar Marshall but north of the Scottish border in Gorgie, Edinburgh, on 31st May 1952 and belonging to Chas G. Dobson Ltd. This is slide valve compound No.85105 of 1929 and registered SY 4079. It had previously belonged to Midlothian County Council.

26. This piston valve compound Marshall spent all its life with the same owner, John E. Nadin of Sheffield. It is No.80730, built in 1926 and registered WB 4857. The photograph was taken in August 1953. (HARRY LUFF)

27. In 1926 Marshalls introduced a radical new design of three-point roller intended for both foundation and surfacing work. It proved too late for capturing the general market but a limited number were produced. The trade name was 'Universal' and this example is West Sussex County Council's No. 49, works No.87635, built in 1935 and registered APX 542. It is under repair at the Council's Drayton Depot near Chichester, on 11th September 1963, a few months before it was acquired for preservation by the then RLS Chairman, H.L. Drewitt, OBE.

28. A drawback in having one's free time at weekends meant that many rollers were then seen parked up at the roadside. This is Robey tandem No.41589 of 1924, registered FE 5953, and is drawn up off the carriageway in The Avenue, Southampton, on Saturday, 21st October 1950. It is No. 11 in the fleet of Limmer & Trinidad Lake Asphalt Co Ltd, a firm which found these rollers particularly useful for asphalt work as they incorporated an agitating device which eliminated the edge marks left by conventional rollers.

29. Another sheeted roller but this one distinctly down at heel and out of use, and also without one of its rear rolls. It is in the Swindon Works yard on 16th March 1952 and is Marshall No.76555, a 12 ton single Q type built in 1923 and registered XO 7892. It is No. 12 in the GWR fleet.

30. A less common make was Ruston & Hornsby and this is one of their slide valve single cylinder rollers, No.52797 of 1920 and registered PB 9748. Belonging to D.I. Williams Ltd, it is working at the site of a new bus station in the centre of Cardiff on 3rd May 1954. It had previously been 'SR1' in Surrey County Council's fleet.

31. There were many Wallis & Steevens rollers to be seen especially in the Southeast. This is one of their modern 'Advance' rollers – No.7837 of 1925, registered HO 6409 and with a living van in tow – and it is proceeding along the main London to Portsmouth A3 road near Petersfield on 13th June 1953. The low height of this design of roller is accentuated by the loftier than usual living van. The pair were then owned by George Ewen Ltd of Petersfield.

32. Wallis & Steevens had introduced their 'Advance' rollers in 1923 and they gained great popularity. Features included twin high pressure cylinders with piston valves, no flywheel for quick reversing and a self-cambering rear axle to accommodate the road profile. This is No.7785, built in 1924 and registered OR 3539. It was photographed in September 1952 and had been owned from new by Willesden Borough Council. (HARRY LUFF)

33. A more conventional and older slide valve single cylinder Wallis & Steevens roller working at Rye House Generating Station, Hertfordshire, on 23rd March 1952. It is No.7128, built in 1911, registered PC 9170 and owned by Herbert Ward & Sons of Egham.

34. Another innovation by Wallis & Steevens was their 3 ton 'Simplicity' design which exercised equal pressure on both rolls and, like the 'Advance', had a self-cambering rear axle. The design had been introduced for a perceived Far Eastern market which did not materialise and only 15 were built. This scene is in London's Old Kent Road on 14th June 1952 and shows No.8023, built in 1932 and registered CG 571, which was owned by Parr-Head & Clements Knowling Ltd.

35. At the earlier rallies it was not unusual for working engines to put in an appearance. This is Henry Woodhams' Ruston & Hornsby compound roller No.115023 at Penshurst rally in Kent on 20th August 1960. The roller was new to this South London firm in 1922 and was registered XM 6373.

36. This working Marshall roller put in an appearance at Paddock Wood rally on 17th August 1957. It belonged to Farrants Ltd of Tunbridge Wells and carried the name "OLD FAITHFUL". It had been built in 1920 as a 5 ton tractor, No.73900, and was sold to Norfolk County Council and registered AH 0823. It was resold in 1923, rebuilt as a roller convertible, and had numerous owners before going to Farrants. It has survived into preservation and is now back in tractor form. Note the registration is incorrectly displayed as 'AH 823'.

37. & 38. Sandwiched between tramcars and a canal this roller has to be in Amsterdam. The photos were taken on 20th May 1953 and at that time steam rollers were quite common in Europe, many being English exports. This particular roller is Aveling & Porter 'O' type No.10792 of 1923 and represents a radical departure from the traditional three-point design. A similar roller is shown in photo 5.

39. Three days later, on 23rd May, this single crank compound roller was seen working in The Hague. It is without a maker's plate and there is a suggestion that it could be Burrell No.2683 built in 1904. However, similar rollers were built by Ruthemeijer in Germany.

40. Many rollers seen in Europe were of continental manufacture. This single cylinder roller is at Pula in Yugoslavia (now in Croatia) on 30th May 1963 and carries the inscription 'Prager Maschinenbau A.G. 9623-1915'. This probably relates to the maker of the boiler and the roller itself appears to be a typical product from the firm of Skoda in Czechoslovakia.

41. With redundant steam rollers on their hands, a number of owners removed or fixed the moving parts and mounted the rollers in playgrounds. This overhead valve compound is Wallis & Steevens No.7449 of 1915, registered KM 9034, and resides in the playground at Portway School, Andover, where it was photographed on 24th January 1976. It had served in France for the WD and was later acquired by Tonbridge UDC. It has since been rescued for preservation and is the only surviving Wallis of this type. (TED CRAWFORTH)

42. Being the home of Eddison it is fitting that Dorchester should have a parked-up member of their fleet. This had been No.398 and is Aveling & Porter 'E' type 10 ton single No.10317, built in 1922 and registered FX 9412.

43. The London Borough of St. Pancras placed their Aveling & Porter 'F' type 10 ton compound roller No.10114 in a playground at Cumberland Market, close by Regent's Park. A few local boys are happily playing on it on Sunday afternoon, 11th October 1953, but their pleasure is not to last.....

44. The Council then decided to build a Wild West adventure park on the site, bringing in tons of fill to create a prairie effect and burying the roller in the process. The mood later changed again and in 1989 a bulldozer was brought in to clear the fill, only to come up hard against a forgotten steam roller. However, and in spite of its incarceration, all was not lost and the roller has been restored – and appropriately named "CUMBERLAND". This photo of the same machine was taken at A.C. Bicknell's yard at Hollycombe, West Sussex, on 21st May 1994. The roller was built in 1921 and registered XD 8230.

THE FAIRGROUND SCENE

45. Very few working showman's engines could be seen after World War II but one was set up for several years at the Vale of Health on Hampstead Heath where it regularly generated for a very run down scenic motor charabanc ride. The engine was Burrell scenic type showman's road locomotive No.3884, built in 1921 and registered XH 5728. It was still with its original owner, Frederick Gray, and carried the name "GLADIATOR" although it had been named "WONDER" in its earliest years. The photo was taken on 14th April 1952 and the inset shows the charabanc ride with makeshift canopy replacing the elaborate proscenium and, further back, a very large and handsome Gavioli organ. The 'scenic type' road locomotive had been adapted from the basic showman's type by adding an auxiliary exciter dynamo, usually just behind the chimney. This enabled the engine's main dynamo to cope with the high starting loads required for the heavy scenic railway cars.

46. One had to go a little further from Central London to see a showman's engine on the road, to Richmond in fact, where an engine regularly worked from Southall to attend bank holiday fairs at Lower Deer Park. This was Sally Beach's "LORD FISHER" which, after three changes of ownership and two changes of name, had been purchased by Miss Beach in 1949. It then took its third name "LORD FISHER" from the earliest member of her fleet. The engine was an 8nhp showman's road locomotive built by Burrells in 1907, No.2894, and registered FK 1463. When this photo was taken at Richmond on 6th August 1951, the engine had, as usual, brought over a set of steam driven galloping horses – see photo 51. Lighting was being provided by an i/c generator hence "LORD FISHER's" dynamo was idle.

47. Burrell No.3967 was built in 1923 as a haulage engine and registered MO 2116. It was purchased by Jacob Studt Jr in 1927, converted to a showman's road locomotive by Charles Openshaw and named "MORNING STAR". It retained the name through two more changes of ownership, the second being to Jos Manning of Buntingford in 1946 and it is seen under his mantle on the road at Potters Bar a year or two later. (DON THOMPSON)

48. The last showman's engine to work commercially in Britain was Charles Presland's "PRINCESS MARY". It is seen at one of its regular calls, the Ship & Shovel, Barking, on 19th April 1954, some four years before its retirement. It is another Burrell, built as a showman's in 1922, numbered 3949 and registered NO 8287. First owned by William Nichols of Forest Gate, it was purchased by Charles Presland of Tilbury in 1943.

49. The best known showman's road locomotives in the immediate post-war years were those of Pat Collins of Bloxwich, Staffordshire. Four were at the Aston Onion Fair on 7th June 1952 with the pair seen here generating for their rides. On the left is "No.1", purchased new in 1920 and built by Burrells as an 8nhp showman's engine and later converted to a scenic type, works No.3865 and registered DH 2507. The other engine is "GOLIATH" of rather more austere appearance and built by McLarens in 1918 as a haulage engine for the WD, works No.1623. It had been acquired by Collins in 1921 who converted it to a showman's engine and gave it its name and obtained the registration number DH 2482. Also present was "LEADER" which features across the page (photo 50) and another Burrell, No.2788 "THE GRIFFIN".

50. A year earlier "LEADER" had attended a fair at Sedgley, between Wolverhampton and Dudley. It was the morning of Sunday, 3rd June 1951, and the fair had already been dismantled – and when I passed by again an hour or so later, everything had gone! The engine is Foster No.14405, built in 1921 as a showman's for J.E. Whiting of Sheffield and then registered WA 5519. It came to Collins in 1927, presumably via Fosters, as it was renumbered 14446 and re-registered DH 4593.

51. This photo was taken on 17th April 1954 and shows the only commercially operated steam driven galloping horses ride then to be seen in the London area. It had been brought to Richmond by "LORD FISHER" (see photo 46); the ride like the engine belonging to Sally Beach. It is a three-abreast set of gallopers built by Savage and driven by the centre engine featured in photo 53.

52. Down on the South Coast, Thomas Smith & Sons of Shoreham operated this Savage built three-abreast ride of cockerels and galloping horses. Still steam driven, Savage engine No.699 drove the ride and a companion engine gave power to the Gaudin organ. Unlike the anti-clockwise movement of Continental and North American rides, the British practice of clockwise rotation enabled sentences to be displayed on the rounding boards. Hence, as time went by, terse statements tended to displace the animated scenes that once graced these roundings. This scene is at Arundel on 9th June 1951.

53. The nameplate "MAY QUEEN" had adorned a traction engine but here it surmounts the centre engine on Sally Beach's gallopers. As with so many rides, galloping horses were mainly developed by Savages Ltd of Kings Lynn who went on to produce most of the centre engines used in this country. Although this photo was taken on 4th August 1952 the ride still exists with centre engine No.627 of 1895 and organ engine No.713 of 1898, but it is not certain whether there have been any changes of either engine over the years.

54. Many showmen retained the centre engines after the installation of electric drive. This is Botton Brothers' electrically operated four-abreast cockerels and galloping horses but it retains its Savage engine No.704 of 1897, named "GENERAL BULLER". Bottons regularly attended the Red House fair on Mitcham Common where this photo was taken on 6th June 1949.

55. Moving forward to the preservation era, we can see better what a centre engine looks like. George Cushing displayed this engine at Raynham rally in Norfolk on 15th September 1962. The single cylinder vertical engine drives the organ – Savage No.418 of 1887 – whilst the twin cylinder horizontal engine seen behind the flywheel – Savage No.421 also of 1887 – drives the ride.

56. In addition to Savages, Tidmans of Norwich and Walkers of Tewkesbury produced centre engines but neither firm gave works numbers to their products. This is a disused Walker engine on a chairoplane ride at a steam working near Thirsk on 1st October 1972. Note the belt driving directly on to the flywheel of the engine.

57. The fair on Hounslow Heath is doing brisk business on 15th April 1952. There are three adult rides; at centre is George Irvin & Sons electric galloping horses with a particularly fine Marenghi organ, while on the right is Percy Cole's Venetian gondola steam operated switchback.

58. & 59. Percy Cole's gondola switchback was built by C.J. Spooner of Burton-on-Trent and was driven by Savage centre engine No.740 of 1898. This was much larger than a gallopers centre engine and the linkage to the rotating cars was centred over the engine's chimney. The extremely ornate appearance of the public side of the ride contrasts with the clutter of its inner workings. The mechanism of the switchbacks was very cumbersome and it was later realised that putting electric motors in the cars would make for substantial savings. The large centre engines and all the linkage could be done away with and the road locomotive used to haul the ride could also be used to drive it. In addition there was a lot of unused space in the centre of the ride and this could be put to good use with elaborate scenic effects, so giving rise to the term 'scenic railway'.

60. The last commercial rides to abandon steam were the giant swing yachts. These were usually mounted in pairs, but each yacht was separately driven. Most were driven by Savage engines, this one is No.867 of 1915. The yachts are Harry Gray's "BIG LIZZIE" and "QUEEN MARY" and are set up at Hampstead Heath on 1st August 1949.

61. A very similar ride but the photo is taken from the front to show the organ rather than from the rear to show the engine's smokebox. These are Joe Ling's unnamed yachts at Wanstead Flats on 19th April 1954 and are operated by Savage engine No.886 of 1921. Some two dozen sets of giant swing yachts were built, the first in 1894 and the last in1928.

62. Harry Lee of Bradford had one of the finest sets of yachts, again driven by a Savage engine but as he owned three separate engines, I am not sure which one is in use here. The yachts were named after America's Cup yacht race contestants "COLUMBIA" and "SHAMROCK", so the underside of the nearer yacht appropriately displays the Union flag. In later years Harry Lee attended preservation era events and his yachts are seen here at the Shottesbrooke Park Steam Fair, near Maidenhead, on 30th August 1964. In fact this was one of only two steam rides present. (See photo 167.)

63. The exception to the 'twin-yacht' rule was G. Ryan & Sons' single yacht "H.M.S. VICTORY", seen here at Sefton Park, Liverpool, on 2nd June 1952. This ride had not been built by Savages but by Fred & Walter Sowden of Bradford. Neither did it have a Savage engine and by 1952 it was driven by the unlikely adaptation of a Burrell single crank compound engine from a steam roller! This was works No.3356 of 1912 and survives in the ride to this day at the Hollycombe Collection in West Sussex. By coincidence, this was the other steam operated ride present at the 1964 Shottesbrooke Park Steam Fair.

64. Just as with roundabouts, it was difficult to see a yacht engine inside a ride but at least with these large portable type engines, they could be seen to advantage when travelling from one site to another. This is the last yacht engine to be built, Savage No.901 of 1928, and it is southbound on the Tyne Bridge, Newcastle, on Sunday, 5th March 1950. It was then owned by the Scottish showman Dan Taylor with the yachts surprisingly named "MISS ENGLAND" and "MISS AMERICA". However he had just sold the ride to the Kursaal Amusement Park at Southend-on-Sea and it was presumably on its way to Essex.

65. The ride was then set up 'permanently' at Southend's Kursaal amusement park and given the name "TUG BOATS". It was quite tastefully adorned with a ship's hull, a bridge and life buoys. It remained here for several seasons but finished up at nearby Maldon as a single yacht ride and with Savage engine No.865. The photograph was taken on a quiet Saturday afternoon, 16th September 1950.

66. On 17th August 1952 the great Mitcham fair had just pulled down and another of Harry Gray's yacht engines is waiting to be moved out. This is not a Savage but Robey No.43886, built in 1927. Its working is very similar to the Savage design and both had a single cylinder for each yacht. Instead of conventional valve gear, each piston rod had a spindle projecting from the cross head, which struck a pivoted lever towards the end of each stroke. The lever in turn operated the steam and exhaust valves, so reversing the piston. The pivoted lever was worked by hand to initiate the swing but as soon as the yacht was under way the gear would work automatically. There were of course no flywheels. The drive to each yacht was imparted by a chain carried round a small pulley fixed to a fulcrum at the top of the ride. The particular shape of the pivoted lever led to its popular description as 'rabbit gear'. No.43886 was the last of a small number of engines and boilers built by Robeys for swing yacht rides.

67. A fascinating type of ride was the 'tunnel railway' although I only managed to see electrified examples in operation and these were on the continent. In essence it was a steam train on a circular track of about 40 feet diameter. It was developed by Savages in the late Victorian period when euphoria for the first Channel Tunnel scheme was at its height, hence the opportunity was taken to put much of the ride in a tunnel. In 1994/95 the Industrial Railway Record estimated that some 14 of these rides were built with the locomotives mostly by Savages but also by John Fowler, Thomas Green and W.G. Bagnall, and they dated from 1879 to 1895. I was fortunate to see what was probably the last surviving locomotive which was then in Harold Goodey's yard at Twyford, Berkshire, on 28th October 1951. The locomotive was a Savage built 2-2-2 tank/tender named "CHAMPION" and built on a curve with converging axles and the outside driving wheel of larger diameter than the inside one. The leading and trailing wheels were loose on their axles and hence of equal diameter. The photo shows the inside elevation of the loco, not visible when the ride was built up. It also shows the rudimentary cab equipment including the steam wheel-valve handle rather than a regulator. The early history of the ride is uncertain but it is thought to have last been operated during World War II by one of the Beach family before ending up in Goodey's yard. Harold Goodey's collection was sold by auction in 1952 and "CHAMPION" does not appear to have survived.

68. At the start of the nineteen-fifties, steam wagons were getting very few and far between but the North Thames Gas Board continued to deliver coke by steam within the inner London suburbs on both sides of the Thames. They used modern Sentinel S4 waggons with their 'four cylinders in line' engines, more akin to automotive practice, and cardan shaft drive. Seen here is fleet number 267 in York Road, Waterloo, on 13th July 1951, with the decorated façade of the 1951 Festival of Britain's South Bank Exhibition as a backdrop. The waggon, Sentinel No.9227, was new to the Gas, Light & Coke Company in 1935 and registered CGW 845.

69. An unmistakable Foden overtype tractor could still be seen in West London. It belonged to Q.M. Camroux & Co Ltd and is at Shepherds Bush coal yard on 27th October 1951 about to pick up coal for Hammersmith Hospital. The trailer has a belt floor operated by two handles hanging on its front wall; no easy task I would think. The tractor is Foden No.13196, built in 1928 and registered GC 5832. It was bought second-hand by Camroux in 1932.

70. An S4 waggon seen on 6th October 1954 delivering beer in Kent. It belonged to the Wingham Engineering Company of Canterbury and was hired out to Fremlins Brewery who had painted it in their customary livery complete with elephant trade mark and given it fleet number 92. It is Sentinel No.9023, built in 1934, registered AKR 958, and has stopped outside the Griffin Inn at Dover.

71. This Sentinel DG6 waggon is at Glossops' Mitcham Depot on 2nd December 1950 and was used for transporting road tar. Built in 1931, works No.8562 and registered FD 6603, it was No.1 in the ownership of Thames Tar Products and Contractors Ltd. It had previously worked for a Midlands firm, hence the Dudley registration.

72. At that time Liverpool was undoubtedly the most likely place to see steam wagons at work. This is Sentinel 'Super' waggon No.6258, built in 1925, registered NE 4569 and numbered 11 in the fleet of Wm. Harper & Sons Ltd. Heavily loaded, and with trailer in tow, it is in The Strand at James Street intersection, close to the Pier Head, on 3rd November 1951. The more rugged older types such as the 'Super' and 'DG' were favoured over the 'S' type for the difficult conditions met with in the Docks.

73. The last wagon produced by the Leeds builder – the Yorkshire Patent Steam Wagon Co Ltd – was No.2271 in 1937. It was delivered to the Sheffield Corporation Electric Supply Dept and registered EWA 116, but by the time the photograph was taken in March 1953 it had been taken over by the nationalised Yorkshire Electricity Board. The Yorkshire firm's distinctive transversely mounted boiler is partly masked by a front apron whilst a vertical compound engine is mounted just behind the driver's seat. (JACK WYSE)

74. The Portsea Island Gas Light Co (Portsmouth Gas Company from 1926) bought seven Foden wagons and the first one to be delivered was still on the active list when photographed at their Hilsea Works on 30th December 1950. It is No.5788, built in 1915 and registered M 8160. It had been retained at the works for internal use and was called upon to take hot coke from the retorts when the regular handling gear was out of action. With nationalisation of the gas industry in 1949, it carried the number 1F bestowed by the Southern Gas Board.

75. Croydon Corporation also retained one of their steam wagons for special duties. With the withdrawal of regular steam haulage during World War II, Foden No.8304 was selected for sterilising pig food bins; these were dustbins in residential streets for householders to place unwanted food scraps. When this duty ceased the wagon filled another important need as a heating plant for the methane plant at Waddon Marsh sewage works. The gas was used to drive many municipal vehicles and so help out scarce oil supplies. The wagon had been built for the War Department in 1918 and was later acquired by the Corporation, registered BY 7646, and numbered 13 in the municipal fleet but later renumbered SW 45. With just its back end protruding from its shanty boiler house, it is seen at the Waddon Marsh methane plant on 8th April 1951.

76. To see what the wagon really looked like, we move forward to 7th August 1961 when it was present at one of the great Woburn rallies. It was then owned by B. A. Pitts of Horley, its third owner since the Corporation sold it in the late nineteen-fifties.

77. Whilst most steel works used railways for internal movements, Brown Bayley Steels Ltd of Attercliffe, Sheffield, employed Sentinel 'Standard' waggons. Seen here is works No.2973, new in 1920, registered AW 6682 and given fleet No. 3. This vehicle along with several similar vintage companions were well suited for this work and remained in service long enough for them to be snapped up for preservation. (See photo 191.) (KEN BARGH)

78. The London County Council Tramways had a large fleet of overtype wagons but these had all been withdrawn by the outbreak of World War II. However, the LCC Tramways had also purchased two gully emptiers from the Yorkshire Patent Steam Wagon Co. These served to flush out and drain the conduit of the Council's unusual current collection system. Built in 1925 they were of typical Yorkshire design and bore works Nos.1510 & 1511. They were registered XX 780 and XX 781 and carried fleet Nos. 17 & 18. With the demise of the North London Tramways, No. 17 was withdrawn in 1939 but No. 18 soldiered on in South London under the London Passenger Transport Board regime until 1948 when it was replaced by an i/c vehicle for the final years of the tramways. (BILL HAYNES)

79. The main users of steam wagons in the early nineteen-fifties were road resurfacing contractors as these vehicles proved eminently suitable for conversion to tar sprayers and road planers, and they avoided the very high taxation levied on their haulage counterparts. This is No.144 in the W. & J. Glossop Ltd fleet and is Sentinel DG4 No.7888, registered MT 3600. It is a tar sprayer with the characteristic rectangular tank of this firm's earlier period and is at their Mitcham Depot on 22nd March 1951. The waggon had been built in 1929 for the Ham River Grit Co.

80. A Glossop crew working on another Sentinel waggon at the depot on the same day. The Mitcham Depot had many derelict waggons around at the time of my visit but there was also a lot of activity with eight active waggons receiving attention. The site was close by Beddington Lane Halt on the West Croydon – Wimbledon line which is now served by Croydon Tramlink. Modern industrial premises have replaced Glossop's motley collection of buildings.

81. This is Glossop's No.169 also photographed on the same day; a tar sprayer with a later elliptical tank, and destined to remain in service until 1965. It is Sentinel DG4 No.8681, built in 1932 and registered GW 2938.

82. A back view of No.169 showing its Worthington/Simpson tar pump carried on the rear framing.

83. Glossop's No.120 was a road planer and is outside the Mitcham Depot on 7th July 1951. Whereas Glossop's London based vehicles were painted black, No.120 displays the Hipperholme, Halifax address and is painted in the maroon livery more generally associated with the firm. The waggon had started life in 1926 as a four wheeled 'Super', works No.6400 and registered BA 5665. It was sold to W. & J. Glossop in 1937 and converted to a tar sprayer but in post-war years rebuilt again, this time to an articulated road planer. The last Sentinel to be used by Glossops was No.8666 (fleet No.106) and when it was reconditioned in the nineteen-sixties it was given No.6400's works plate. It still carries this plate in preservation.

84. The last photo in this Glossop selection shows their tar sprayer No. 171 inside the repair shop at Mitcham. This DG4 waggon dated from 1930, had works No.8385, and carried a more modern style of lettering on the apron front but few others were so adorned, and the background colour was still the customary London black.

85. Sentinels by no means monopolised the road surfacing fleets. Here is Foden rigid six-wheeler No.13156 of 1928, registered UR 1328, and belonging to the Penmaenmawr & Trinidad Lake Asphalt Co Ltd. It served as an asphalt mixer and operated in the Liverpool area. The firm also used portables belted up to asphalt mixers, probably the last portables to be used in an urban environment. (DON THOMPSON)

86. Leaving just enough room for the tram to squeeze by, this similar Foden 3-axle wagon of the Penmaenmawr company is working at Lord Street in the centre of Liverpool on Sunday morning, 4th November 1951. It is No. 13008, registered TU 9235 and, like 13156, was built in 1928. It also carries a large asphalt boiler with mechanical agitation. The wagon has survived but has lost its registration number and now carries SS 9191 plates.

87. The Yorkshire firm, D. Wood & Co Ltd of Yeadon, included two Yorkshire wagons in their fleet. This one has been adapted as a tar-sprayer from wagon No.2189, which had been built in 1932 for Bradford Corporation. It is parked up at Stockton on the Forest near York in July 1952. (PETER WILLIAMS)

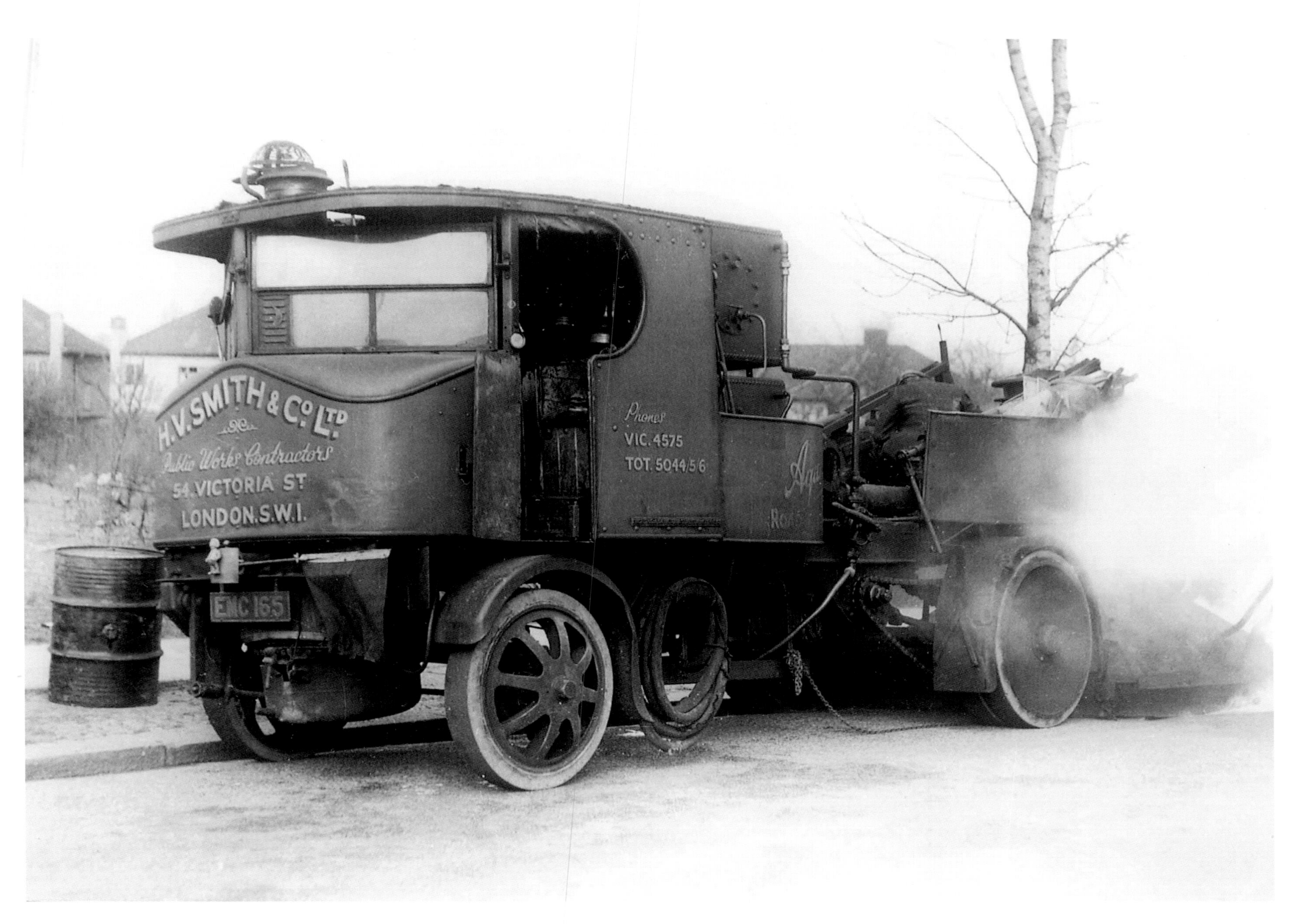

88. Reverting to Sentinels, this is 'Super' waggon No.6606, built in 1926, supplied to Goodman & Tidy in Bermondsey and registered YU 771. When converted to a road planer for the Tottenham firm of H.V. Smith & Co Ltd it was re-registered EMC 165 and is seen working in this mode at New Southgate. (DON THOMPSON)

89. Another of H.V. Smith's acquisitions was Sentinel DG4 No.8454 and as a tar-sprayer is at work near London Airport in February 1955. It had been built in 1931 as a 3-way tipper for the Wrekin Coal Company Ltd, Shropshire, and registered UX 7958. It was sold to Smiths in 1935 who converted it to a tar sprayer and re-registered it CML 734. (John Meredith collection)

90. Sentinel 8454 survived into preservation and after several changes of ownership, was rebuilt by Peter Bowers into the type of waggon once operated by the grain merchants, James & Son. The firm had a highly noticeable yellow livery with red lettering and a distinctive body shape. It is seen here on 29th August 2002 at the Great Dorset Steam Fair. Note the original registration – UX 7958 – has been restored. It may be questioned whether this artificial identity is justified but we now have a glimpse from the past of a well known and attractive fleet.

A MISCELLANY

The first three sections have been devoted to the more familiar use of steam in the urban scene but the next few photographs illustrate some unusual uses that could be seen.

91. The steam tractor was becoming extremely rare but match manufacturers Bryant & May Ltd used a pair of tractors at their East London factory for hauling timber logs from the nearby River Lee Navigation. The photograph shows Foster 'Wellington' tractor No. 14509, registered YM 3490, and built ca 1920. Their second tractor was Burrell No.3576 built in 1914 and registered HO 5900. The scene is dated 25th August 1951 after the engines had ceased to be used and they are thought to have been broken up soon afterwards.

92. Another tractor survived in the ownership of Coulsdon & Purley UDC. This is Aveling & Porter No.12186 of 1928, registered PK 2684, and it continued in use, towing a tar boiler, for several years after World War II. It was later sold to C.W. Lambert of Horsmonden and can be seen today at the Thursford Museum. (REV NORMAN LEMPRIÈRE)

93. Folkestone Waterworks purchased Allchin traction engine No.1173 as late as 1951 to provide an emergency source for lifting equipment from their wells. It is a 6 nhp engine built in 1901 and registered KE 1984, and it is being driven by Mr Reynolds, secretary of the company, who must have been an enthusiast as the Allchin was taken to many rallies. On this occasion it is at the Pegden Brothers rally at Elham on 30th July 1955. The engine was not sold until 1981 and still exists bearing the name "AQUARIUS".

94. Northampton County Borough purchased McLaren 8 nhp road locomotive No.1713 in 1940 and fitted it with a crane for dealing with wartime incidents such as bombings and crashed aircraft. It had previously belonged to the local firm of Smith's Timber Co, hence its Northampton registration NH 3998, and had been bought new in 1922. It was tucked well inside the Borough's depot at St James when photographed on 14th July 1951. It survives but, unsurprisingly, the crane has been removed and it has been converted to a showman.

95. There were a number of railway depots and yards where shunting was performed by horses or i/c tractors but shunting by road steam vehicles was exceptionally rare. However it was performed for many years by the Teignmouth Quay Co Ltd who had purchased this 5 ton Sentinel 'Super Tractor' in 1925 and named it "THE ELEPHANT". It bore works number 5644 but, with its work restricted to the firm's premises, it was not registered until it was given 757 CTT in the post-war period. "THE ELEPHANT" was sold in 1963 and is now preserved in Holland. (DON THOMPSON)

96. There was no back-up for "THE ELEPHANT" until 1933 when a new Sentinel S4 waggon arrived. This was No.8850 and was registered FJ 9248, and it too continued in operation until 1963, although without fenders it was not as versatile for wagon shunting as its companion. The S4 was named "THE LION" and also survives in preservation. The photograph is dated 21st June 1961.

97. A few industrial concerns used conversions from road to rail for shunting railway wagons. This usually had limited success due to their low weight and low speed. Perhaps the greatest exponent was the Derbyshire Carriage & Wagon Co Ltd of New Whittington, near Chesterfield, who operated four such locomotives post World War II. In fact this, their most sophisticated conversion, did not appear until 1951; it consists of the boiler and engine of Ruston Proctor 'Lincoln Imp' tractor No.52337, dating from 1918, mounted on a wagon underframe. With chain drive to the rear axle and another chain between the two axles, the locomotive ran as an 0-4-0 but the second chain was later discarded so reducing it to a 2-2-0. (IAN DAVIDSON)

98. The firm's three other locomotives were relatively straight-forward conversions – the two shown here are based on Garrett No.34181 of 1922 (left) and Foden No.13152 of 1928 (right). There was also an 0-4-2 locomotive based on Sentinel waggon No.7973, a DG6 of 1929. Very few other conversions could be seen after World War II; the Phoenix Ironworks of Leicester was one location, where converted Foden wagon No.12070 survived until 1951. (John Meredith collection)

99. Many steam road locomotive builders tried their hand at producing "traction engine" style railway locomotives based on their road designs and components. Far and away the most successful was Aveling & Porter whose numbers built ran well into three figures and examples could be seen working in various parts of Britain up to the nineteen-fifties. The initial design incorporated a chain drive and this developed into a 2-2-0 geared locomotive which was produced during the last quarter of the nineteenth century. An 0-4-0 design then took over but strangely a final example of the 2-2-0 design was built in 1926 and proved to be the very last locomotive produced by Avelings. This locomotive was No.9449 and was delivered to the Holborough Cement Co just four miles up the River Medway from the builder's works. It is seen under repair on 8th April 1950 and it will be noted that the front buffer beam has had to be removed to gain access to the smokebox and tubes. The locomotive still exists as the sole survivor of the 2-2-0 type, yet there have been sacrilegious suggestions that it be converted to a road loco!

100. The final and more numerous 0-4-0 geared locomotive design was in production from 1893 to 1925 with this one, No.6158, dating from 1906. It had originally been operated by Gypsum Mines Ltd at Mountfield, East Sussex, hence the name "SIRAPITE" but it latterly served as works shunter at the Richard Garrett Engineering Works at Leiston, Suffolk, where it was photographed on 19th December 1961. Note the Kentish white horse has been replaced by a Garrett panther. The locomotive survives but is in a run down condition although it has recently been returned to Leiston where it is housed at the Garrett Long Shop Museum.

101. Among other traction engine builders supplying locomotive was Marshalls who built just two, and one of them, No.6402 dating from 1878, was delivered to Pepper & Son's lime works at Amberley, West Sussex. This was an undertype and is parked inside its shelter on 28th April 1951.

102. The Marshall was then being used as stand-by; the regular locomotive being another Aveling & Porter 0-4-0, No.4371 built in 1899. This was also photographed on 28th April 1951 and it too spent its entire working life at Amberley. The lime works site is now occupied by the acclaimed Chalk Pits Museum; it is unfortunate that neither the Marshall nor the Aveling have survived to form part of their collection.

103. The most successful combination of road and rail steam production was by Sentinels, their rail vehicles including shunting locomotives and passenger railcars. Both incorporated similar boilers and engines to their road counterparts. Their railcars were exported widely but the units for home use lasted only until 1948 when the last of many cars supplied to the LNER was withdrawn. It was a different story with the shunting locomotives and they were still in widespread use well into the nineteen-fifties. This is a 3ft gauge example working for the London Brick Company at Fletton near Peterborough on 14th September 1960. It is named "NUTTY" and was supplied by Sentinels in 1929, works No.7701, and it now forms part of the collection at the Narrow Gauge Museum, Tywyn, Gwynedd.

104. This standard gauge Sentinel is at William Cory's Rochester Coal Wharf on the Medway on 18th April 1950. It is No.7060 dating from 1927 and carries the name "WOOLWICH". Although one of the builder's standard designs it is hardly attractive but the appearance was markedly improved in later versions.

THE RURAL SCENE

105. The use of steam power in the countryside had diminished far more rapidly than in urban areas and it was almost extinct at the end of World War II. However a few ploughing engines were still in use on heavy soils. The most notable operator was John Patten of Little Hadham, Herts, and this is his Fowler Class AA7 18 nhp engine No.15362, built in 1919, registered NK 985 and named "LION". It was paired with No.15363 "TIGER", registered NK 989. (DON THOMPSON)

106. "LION" viewed from the rear and showing the chains that such engines carried. These chains, of several different sizes, were used in all sorts of situations when a direct pull was impossible. Note too the spuds on the rear wheels which provided extra grip. The engine in this instance appears to be cultivating rather than ploughing; ploughing engines also undertook harrowing and mole drainage. These two scenes were taken near Thaxted in about 1950. John Patten's engines were eventually sold in 1960 and many of them survive in preservation, including "LION" and "TIGER"- but they are not the only ploughing engines with these names! (DON THOMPSON)

107. Another working Fowler ploughing engine; this is No.14047, a Class K7 built in 1914 and sold to J.& H. Broome, Inkberrow, Worcs. It was registered CMO 639, presumably after transfer to Lunnicks Ltd of Reading under whose ownership it appears here. The photo was taken at Oakley, Hants., on Sunday, 8th October 1950 when the engine was spotted some 200 yards from the road. It was certainly not in steam at the weekend and with sheeting over the motion it may not have been used for some time. There was no sign of its partner or its tackle.

108. Although Fowlers had a near monopoly of the steam ploughing trade a few other makers did produce ploughing engines. This is Aveling & Porter No.7445 dating from 1911 and lying out of use at the Maidstone yard of H. H. Naylor on 20th August 1951. It was registered KR 4257 and carried the name "KING GEORGE". Its partner – No.7446, KR 4258, "QUEEN MARY" – stood nearby.

109. In those days it was more usual to spot pairs of ploughing engines out of use, generally drawn up side by side. This typical pair is at Crays Hill, Essex, on 24th November 1951 with the owner, G. A. Keeling, standing between them. They are Fowler Class BB 14 nhp engines Nos.13481 (left) and 13482, which were new to the Keeling family in 1913 and later registered NO 796 and NO 797 respectively. Both remain in preservation having had several owners including Construction & Excavation (Tettenhall) Ltd as also mentioned in the caption to photo 110.

110. A few ploughing engines continued in use commercially after their demise in agriculture; the reason was lake dredging. This is 1918 built Fowler Class K7 10 nhp engine No.14695, registered MA 5129, at work at Bramley, Hants., on 16th October 1965. This engine was named "HILDA" although its partner, No. 14694, was not named, and they were then operated by Construction & Excavation (Tettenhall) Ltd.

111. An unsuccessful attempt was made in about 1949 to adapt a Fowler ploughing engine for use as a road planer. The engine concerned was Class BB No.14350, built in 1916 and registered NM 360, but at some stage, in company with its partner No.14349, the pair of engines had their registrations transposed with another pair and henceforth 14350 became NM 363.
Esmond Kimbell purchased the engine and in conjunction with T. T. Boughton undertook the experiment at the latter's Amersham Common premises. A grading blade was rigged up in place of the winding drum, additional gearing was provided to enable the engine to move very slowly and a heating system was installed for using steam from the boiler to soften the tar before grading. Despite such a large boilered engine the heating capacity was insufficient to heat the tar effectively and the experiment was abandoned. The photo was taken at Amersham Common on 12th August 1951. The initials 'BRM' chalked on the smokebox refer to the racing cars that were achieving fame at that time!

112. Steam threshing in postwar Britain was a rarity but just a few outposts continued the practice. This animated scene was recorded on C.W. Buxton's farm at Ufford, Suffolk, in 1949 with Garrett tractor No.32860, built in 1916, and registered BJ 3070. The engine and tackle were owned by H.J. Holland & Sons of Wickham Market. (BOB PRATT)

113. The more familiar sight was to see such agricultural engines out of use as in this photograph. Nonetheless this is a rare make of engine – a Fyson from Soham, in Cambridgeshire. The firm made only 17 traction engines (plus one portable) and this is the last one, No. T17 dating from 1924. It is seen at Burwell, just 4 miles from Soham, on 8th June 1951. No Fyson engine has survived into preservation.

PRESERVATION – THE BEGINNING

114. Chris Lambert of Horsmonden, Kent, was perhaps the first person to seriously promote the preservation of steam road locomotives. Inheriting the family transport and engineering business started by his grandfather, he not only amassed considerable knowledge and practical experience of steam road traction but in his later years he built up a collection of engines with the aim of saving them for posterity. He was also keen to encourage engine enthusiasts and he would hold a 'steam party' at his yard in June each year and would steam as many of his engines as possible. I was privileged to attend these parties in 1952 and 1953 and this is part of the scene that greeted me on the second occasion, 20th June 1953.
The engine on the extreme right is Burrell road locomotive No. 3799 whilst the traction engine in the centre sporting the Kentish horse on the smokebox is Aveling & Porter No.9010. The little engine on the far left is E.L. Wicks' Tasker tractor No.1318 which also appears in photo 116.

115. In another part of the yard, also in 1953, was this well turned out Aveling & Porter overhead valve compound No.4561 of 1900, registered KE 3775 and carrying the name "JIMMY".
Sadly Chris Lambert died just two years later and his engines, then amounting to 30 in number, had to be sold. A few were disposed of privately but 25 changed hands at an auction on 15th June 1955. Luckily the preservation era had commenced and no less than 23 of the 30 still survive, including this Aveling. The main difference from today's auctions was that the maximum bid was then £300 and most of the engines were secured for less than £100 apiece – this one, would you believe, achieved just £85.

116. By the early nineteen fifties there were a few enthusiasts around who had purchased engines and the Horsmonden parties gave owners in the surrounding area a chance to put their engines on display. This is E.L. Wicks' Tasker 'Little Giant' tractor No.1318 of 1906 and registered AA2143. In the right background, the portly gentleman with the trilby hat is Chris Lambert.

117. Another visitor in the yard is this Burrell tractor No.4072, new in 1927 and registered PH 2900. It is being driven by its then owner, Bill Martin of Maidstone.

118. During the steam parties, engines were taken out on to the village streets and to overcome licensing problems, two engines in steam would be coupled together and operated on a single pair of trade plates - not very visible in this instance as the plate is partly obscured by the spud pan. The scene portrays a rare combination of a Davey Paxman (No.19413 of 1916) leading an Allchin (No.3251 of 1925) with both engines thought to be the last ones built by their respective manufacturers. RLS member Maurice Lawson Finch is steersman on the Davey Paxman.

119. Another 'visiting engine', although it was then normally stabled at Horsmonden, is Clayton & Shuttleworth traction engine No.36336 of 1904 and registered BP 5821. It has just come under the Hawkhurst branch railway bridge with Horsmonden station on the left. The entrance to Lambert's yard is on the opposite side of the road. The engine is being driven by its owner, Michael Pink of Ashford.

120. Only some 12 miles from Horsmonden was H.H. Naylor & Sons' yard at Maidstone, but this presented a very different appearance with uncared for engines, some deep in the undergrowth. The collection included a venerable survivor - Aveling & Porter single cylinder traction engine No.721 built in 1871. This is how it appeared on 20th August 1951 although at that time the Road Locomotive Society was already in negotiation for its purchase for preservation.

121. Following purchase by the Society the engine was restored by Aveling-Barford and in 1954 it was presented to the South Kensington Science Museum. It is still prominently displayed there and over fifty years later it remains the only road locomotive appearing in the Museum. Note that the unauthentic brass capuchoned chimney seen in photo 120, and probably taken from a railway locomotive, has been replaced by one of appropriate pattern.

122. 1951 was probably the most important year in the transition from commercial use to preservation. It also occasioned the Festival of Britain which helped to transform the Country from the aftermath of wartime austerity to a period of peacetime expansion. Hardly surprisingly, no steam road locomotives appeared in London's great South Bank Exhibition, although two brand new steam railway locomotives were prominently displayed there, but the Festival encouraged activities and developments all over Britain which included aspects of our road locomotive heritage. A good example was at Ruckinge near Ashford in Kent, where the Festival was commemorated by erecting attractive signs at the approaches to the village honouring prominent former resident, Thomas Aveling.
The partnership of Aveling & Porter set up their works at Rochester in Kent and in the eighteen-sixties they adopted the County of Kent's rampant horse surmounting the inscription 'Invicta' as their trademark. This became an instantly recognisable feature on the smokebox door or headstock of their engines.

123. Although not related to the Festival, this photo was taken only a few days before its opening, and reflects the affection that people felt for the homely steam roller. The scene is in London Road, Tooting Junction, on 27th May 1951, with a typical London Transport bus of the period passing by – a Daimler utility.

124. At Thetford a local Festival Exhibition appropriately included the attendance of two Burrell showman's road locomotives. This one is scenic engine No.3912 "DRAGON", registered CO 4485 and delivered in 1921 to Anderton & Rowland and later operated by Sam Smart & Sons, both firms being based at Bristol. In 1948 the engine was acquired by Jesse Vines of Hardwicke, Gloucestershire, for preservation. Mr Vines was a skilled and enthusiastic engineman and made the well over 300 miles round trip with "DRAGON" to attend the Thetford Festival, and for good measure, included a visit to King's Lynn.

125. The second Burrell seen at Thetford is No.3343. It had been built in 1911 as a road locomotive and was used in the Borders Region around Jedburgh until 1922. It was then returned to East Anglia and converted to a showman's engine for Herbert Stocks of Ipswich. He named it "PRINCESS MARY" and it was given the local registration DX 3441. The engine was subsequently purchased for preservation by A. Phoenix, a one-time Burrell employee, and was entered at the Festival by 'The Steam Engine Preservation Association'. Both engines appear in shabby external condition, so unlike the preservation scenes of later years. The photographs were taken on the 8th June 1951.

126. Although road locomotives were no longer being produced, the reputation manufacturers gained from achievements in their design and construction would put them in good stead. Hence the display of this 1882 built Aveling & Porter roller on the Aveling-Barford Ltd stand at the International Construction Equipment Exhibition at Crystal Palace would assure potential customers that they were dealing with a reputable and experienced firm. The roller is a 10 ton single, works No.1760, and was supplied new to Reading Corporation. In due course it was given Reading registration DP 3672 and was later owned by John Allen & Ford Ltd. It was reportedly used in the construction of the M1 Motorway in 1959. The photo was taken on the 24th June 1961.

127. This ploughing engine is performing a similar task at the 1963 International Construction Equipment Exhibition. It is seen at the same location on 5th July of that year. The engine belonged to John Allen & Sons (Oxford) Ltd and had been built by them in 1913, works No.67 and registered BW 4613.

128. One of the most important events to kick-start traction engine rallying was the Nettlebed Race. This occurred on Sunday, 24th June 1951 when Arthur Napper of Appleford, having challenged a local owner to race with their respective traction engines in the previous year, was himself challenged by Giles Romanes of Maidenhead. Nettlebed, Berkshire, more or less the half way point between the two contestants, was chosen as the venue and the prize would be a firkin of beer. The press then got hold of the story and this assured a good attendance! Here we see Arthur Napper, with the cap, on "OLDTIMER" and his steersman, Dick Blackwell, with trilby, just before the race. The engine is Marshall No.37690, of 6 nhp, registered BH 7373, and dates from 1902.

129. The race involved an out and back course across a large field and this is the outward leg with "OLDTIMER" on the left and Giles Romanes' "EILEEN" on the right. The latter is Wallis & Steevens 7 nhp traction engine No.7683 built in 1919 and registered BL 795. "EILEEN" later flagged a little hence "OLDTIMER" was the winner, but this did not prevent Giles Romanes being summoned for illegally driving his engine to Nettlebed under an agricultural licence and incurring a £5 fine. However the publicity from the further press coverage was of far greater value than the fine, and the engine was thenceforward known as "EILEEN THE ERRING".

130. Stirred on by the enthusiasm at Nettlebed, Arthur Napper organised a more ambitious race at his Bridge Farm, Appleford, in the following year which included a flat race with five engines. This was on Sunday, 8th June 1952 and we can see four of the five engines at the start of the race. From left to right are Giles Romanes' "EILEEN THE ERRING", Miles Chetwynd-Stapleton's "LADYGROVE" (Aveling & Porter No.8923), Esmond Kimbell's "KIM" (Marshall No.69326) and , in the lead, Arthur Napper's "OLDTIMER". The fifth contestant was the Quick Brothers' "PANDORA" (Wallis & Steevens No.7293) and, although suffering problems at the start, it did 'move up the field' but once again "OLDTIMER" was the winner.
Although the event was advertised as a 'race meeting' five other non-contestant engines took part including a Burrell showman's road locomotive (see photo 150).

131. Esmond Kimbell on the left, with steersman Harold Lines is getting "KIM" ready for the race – and note the large gathering that has come along to watch. Mr Kimbell has been a long standing and influential member of the Road Locomotive Society and, as this book is being prepared, we are pleased to offer him our congratulations on reaching his centenary.

132. The stage has now been set for rallying to begin in earnest but the dangers of flat racing were immediately apparent and this practice was not repeated. Engines were still lowly priced and plentiful and there was little incentive to spend large sums of money on them if any major breakage or defect occurred. Hence quite a number that appeared at early rallies later succumbed to the breakers. This is Fowler No.11822, built in 1909 and originally used at a Berkshire brickworks. In 1929 it was purchased by George Baker of Southampton, converted to a showman's road locomotive, named "KING EDWARD" and registered TR 7644. Following further moves it was bought by Arthur Napper in 1954 who kept it for just two years and only two years after that, in 1958, it was broken up, the boiler being in very poor condition. This is the scene at Andover rally on 14th May 1955.

133. This is another Fowler showman's road locomotive but this one is still very much with us. It was built in 1920 as a Class R3 haulage engine for F. Barnes for work in the Portland stone quarries, works No.15657, and given Dorset registration number FX 6661. In 1932 it was returned to Fowlers for conversion to a showman's road locomotive and was then operated by Mrs Oadley of Alfreton, Derbyshire, who named it "KITCHENER". John Crawley acquired it for preservation in 1955 and it is seen at the Woburn Park rally on the 4th August 1958. In 1963 the engine came into much greater prominence when it took a starring role in the film 'The Iron Maiden' and which has given the engine its current name.

134. Rallies quickly established a routine but this did not stop entrants adopting unusual behaviour. Top hats and light clothing were hardly de rigueur for engine crews although the bell carried on the forecarriage of this engine might have had some practical use on a crowded rally field. The engine is J.T. Beeby's "ENTERPRISE", a Clayton & Shuttleworth 7 nhp single No.44103, built in 1911 and registered AL 9348. It is at Kegworth rally on 23rd July 1955.

135. All but the smallest rallies would include a grand parade with broadcast announcements giving details of the engines as they passed the commentator. This is the parade at Elham rally in Kent on the 30th July 1955 with Pegden Brothers' nicely turned out Aveling & Porter 8 nhp overhead valve compound engine No.3387 of 1894 nearest the camera. This engine had spent almost all its working life in Kent yet for reasons unknown it was not registered until the autumn of 1945 when it was issued with HKJ 817.

136. All manner of contrived events were held to entertain the public: musical chairs, egg & spoon races and slow races were among the regular features. Especially popular were the ladies invitation steering races and here Jack Wharton is instructing a young lady at Woburn Park on 7th August 1961. The engine is his 6 nhp single cylinder Marshall No.15391 dating from 1887 and registered BW 5249.

137. Another popular event was the tug of war and two similar sized Foden tractors are in action at Andover on the 1st May 1954. On the right is No.13358 of 1929, owned by Ian Woollett and registered DF 8187 whilst its opponent is Barnet & Howell's "MIGHTY ATOM" of 1932, works No.14078 and registered MJ 369. Unsurprisingly the result was a draw!

138. Such a distinctive engine as this hardly needs the addition of a ship's siren to make it stand out from the crowd. It had been the works crane engine for Ransomes, Sims & Jefferies at their Ipswich plant and had been built by them in 1920, works No.31066 and registered PV 4943. Following its 'productive' career, it spent some time in 'destructive' mode at the scrap yard of J.W. Hardwick & Sons of Ewell, Surrey, where few of the many engines that went in were ever to emerge. No.31066 was an exception and was used by Hardwicks to assist in their trade. It is seen subsequently at the Woburn Park rally on the 7th August 1961 in the ownership of A.G. Evans & Son of Wigginton, Herts.

139. An unheard of proposition today but this engine might have been yours if you had purchased a five shillings (25 pence) draw ticket at the Appleford rally on the 14th June 1958. It is Wallis & Steevens single cylinder engine No.7498, built in 1916 and registered HO 5629. The engine was donated by Mr E.W. Edney of Horndean who was then the Treasurer of the young and almost penniless National Traction Engine Club as a fund raising event. The engine had been built to the order of the Ministry of Munitions and was disposed of to Frederick Allen of Oakley, Hants. By 1941, after a further two owners in Hampshire, it was purchased by James Penfold of Arundel and named "PROGRESS". Mr Edney acquired the engine in 1957 and it appears to have been won by D. Paine of Croydon who certainly acquired the engine in 1958.

140. Most rallies took place in rural surroundings but on Sunday, 20th May 1962, one took place in the centre of Birmingham. Among the engines present was James Dakin's 1910 6 nhp Foster No.12539, registered MA 5730 and named "WINNIE". The smokebox door plate has the tank motif so it has presumably come from a later engine – see the comments accompanying photo 178.

141. Other entrants that day included S.L. Wedgwood & Sons pair of wagons seen here: 'Standard' Sentinel No.2307 of 1919, registered AW 4693 assisting Foden No.5218 of 1915, registered M7287 and later named "GWENNIE WILLAN". Arthur Wedgwood is driving the Foden and he later drove it extensively on a promotional campaign for Halls Mentholyptus cough sweets.

The entrance to Birmingham's former Museum of Science and Industry in Newhall Street can be seen between the two wagons. Although rather cramped, it provided a more satisfying experience for steam enthusiasts than its modern and sanitised replacement, the Think Tank Museum in Curzon Street.

142. In the 1950s there were still many laid-up engines across the country and, if in reasonable condition, there was a good chance of rescue. This is Fred Harris & Sons' "SWEET NOTHING", Burrell No.2879, built in 1907 and registered NO 698, and seen at Ashington, West Sussex, on the 24th June 1956.

143. Only two years later the same engine is to be seen at Woburn Park rally on the 4th August 1958 in the ownership of E.W. Gale of Whittlesey near Peterborough and now carries the name "PRINCESS ROYAL". In its earliest days it had been owned by Essex showman Henry Thurston and was then named "LORD NELSON" whilst both "SWEET NOTHING" and "PRINCESS ROYAL" were names bestowed by Fred Harris.

144. On 23rd October 1953 and only some 25 miles from Ashington – at Buckland, Reigate, Surrey – we see Wantage 8 nhp engine No.1389, built in 1900, registered PB 9722, and with its owner, F.J. Sanders. The engine had been with the family since new and Mr Sanders was reluctant to let it go but he died soon afterwards and the engine was sold for preservation.

145. The purchaser was J. Hutchens of Ferndown, Dorset, who restored the engine and gave it the name "CONSTANCE". It is seen opening the Beaulieu rally on 21st May 1961 with Lord Montagu on the footplate.

146. The previous two out of use engines had remained with their commercial owners but there were several more engines to be found in dealers' yards. One of the more interesting yards was at Twyford, Berkshire, where Harold Goodey had a veritable Aladdin's Cave of old equipment and vehicles including several traction engines. This scene was taken on Boxing Day 1951 and from left to right the three showman's road locomotives are Foster No.12504 "KING GEORGE V", Burrell No.2701 "BLACK PRINCE" and Burrell No.3804 "INDEPENDENCE". In 1952 the whole collection was put up for sale and although the Foster went for scrap, the two Burrells were sold for preservation. (See also photo 67.)

147. This is "BLACK PRINCE" some 15 years later, on 28th August 1966, in the collection of Alan Bloom at Bressingham, Norfolk. It had been built as a haulage engine in 1904 but was converted to a showman's road locomotive in the late 1930s for London showman Harry Gray. It carries Surrey registration PE 7181.

148. The last of this quartet of 'then & now' photographs features Thornycroft wagon No. 39, built in 1900, registered AD 115 and named "DOROTHY". It is seen in John Crawley's ownership and prior to its restoration, at the Woburn Park rally on the 4th August 1958.

149. Restoration of the Thornycroft was undertaken by Robert H. Crawford of Boston, Lincolnshire and No.39 is now seen on the 28th August 1977 at 'Expo'77' on the Peterborough show ground.

150. The first showman's road locomotive to appear at a rally was Burrell No. 3489 "KING GEORGE VI"; this was at the Appleford race meeting on 8th June 1952. No.3489 had been built in1913 for J. Hickey & Sons of Richmond, Surrey, as a haulage engine. It was named "CITY OF LONDON" and given Surrey registration PB 9624. When Hickeys turned to internal combustion vehicles in the 1930s, "CITY OF LONDON" was converted to showman's type and in its new guise was used firstly in the London area by Swales Bolesworth and then in Kent by Ted Andrews. Unsurprisingly it received its name change under its Kentish owner! It was purchased for preservation by S.J. (Jack) Wharton of Witney, Oxfordshire, who restored it and then maintained it in excellent condition, both mechanically and in appearance.

151. The ultimate in the Fowler range of showman's road locomotives was "SUPREME". It had been built in 1934, works No.20223, for Mrs A. Deakin & Son of Brynmawr, South Wales, and carries Brecon registration EU 5313. Following its showland career it achieved fame in Glasgow as one of Road Engines & Kerr's fleet, hauling locomotives from the North British Locomotive Works to the Docks. It was purchased for preservation in 1951 and driven from Glasgow to Chichester, West Sussex, but for reasons unknown the project failed and it was sold to J.W. Hardwick & Sons, West Ewell, Surrey. It languished in Hardwick's yard in deplorable condition until purchased in 1958 by Jack Wharton. He then undertook the major task of restoration which, according to his Presidential Address to the Road Locomotive Society in 1971, took 12 years and 20,000 hours of work. The successful outcome is here on display at the Leeds & District Traction Engine Club's rally at Harewood on the 31st August 1970.

152. Getting to rallies in the early days frequently involved driving engines along the generally quieter roads of that time. G.L. Tribe of Bratton Fleming, Devon, undertook a 40 mile round trip to attend the Umberleigh rally on 6th June 1964 and as a white gloved constable looks on, he turns off the A377 to cross over the River Taw to get to the rally ground. This Aveling & Porter 6 nhp compound is named "GRANDSIRE", works No.6407 and carries local registration TA 2759. It was built in 1907.

153. Attending the Andover rally on 14th May 1955 presented few problems for local engine owner Derek Marder, or for other drivers sharing that road. The engine is Garrett tractor No.30159, new in 1912, named "VICTORIA" and registered BJ 1206.

155. This Robey tractor is passing through Tadcaster, West Riding of Yorkshire, on 24th August 1967. Its owner 'Duke' Brewer from Pickering spent much of the summer months travelling between rallies with trailer and caravan, and indeed his supportive wife. Named "VILLAGE QUEEN" and registered FE 5043, the engine was built in 1915, works No.33957. However the 5043 registration dates from 1922 when Robeys rebuilt the engine as 40798 but it is carrying its original plate. It has since reverted to its original Lincoln registration, FE 1620. The 'steam motor' or 'tractor' came into being as a result of the 1898 Highways Act which, among other things, permitted engines of up to 3 tons to be driven by one man. This was amended in 1903 and permitted engines of up to 5 tons. The 1898 act also introduced vehicle licensing using index marks or registration numbers that are still familiar today. Any vehicle over 5 tons was still subject to the old County licensing system and did not require the display of registration indexes but these vehicles were brought into line in 1921.

154. Another quiet road sees Burrell 7 nhp traction engine No. 2421 making its way from Bunny, Nottinghamshire, to Kegworth Carnival, Leicestershire, on 23rd July 1955, a journey of less than 10 miles. The Burrell, a single cylinder engine, belonged to W.H. Dorman and was new in 1901. It carries the name "OLD GLORY" and is registered EB 3051.

156. J. W. Hardwick & Sons of Ewell, Surrey, had long been involved with the disposal of engines. However as preservation became widespread many of the engines we see today passed through their hands and the firm also took a part in active preservation. This is their Foster showman's road locomotive No.14632, built in 1934, registered AAU 370 and named "SUCCESS" by its first owners, Hibble & Mellors of Nottingham. It is making an appearance at the first Andover rally on 6th April 1953. The 50 mile journey from Ewell had been made on this low loader and, with very poor ground conditions on the rally field, I don't think it got very far from its trailer.

157. Another Andover visitor, this time on the 14th May 1955, was J. H. Dingle's Garrett tractor No.33987, built in 1920 and registered BJ 5597. Like "SUCCESS" it had been brought to the rally on a low loader but in this instance a considerably longer journey of nearly 200 miles was involved, from Kelly Bray just across the River Tamar in Cornwall.

158. It wasn't long before the games indulged in at the earlier rallies were supplemented by more serious pursuits such as practical demonstrations of the work the engines performed. This is nominally the East Anglian Traction Engine Club's engine. It is Burrell No.3112, a 7 nhp single crank compound dating from 1909, registered CF 3440, and is drawing a threshing machine on to the rally field at Saling, Essex, on 9th July 1955. It was intended that the engine would be used by Club members to gain experience but in fact it was owned by Gerald Dixon of Sudbury.

159. Moving north to Sutton-on-the-Forest, near York, a Steam Working was staged on 15th September 1973. A. Raley's 7 nhp Wallis & Steevens single No.7774 of 1923, registered CT 6081, is driving a Foster 54" drum threshing machine and a trusser, the latter probably by Ruston & Hornsby. It would appear that there are problems with the operation of the trusser, a not so unusual occurrence I am told, even in commercial days.

160. Another Yorkshire steam working, this time at Birdforth Farm near Thirsk on the 2nd October 1973, and E.M. Meadowcroft's Marshall No.49725 is driving a stone crusher. The engine, a 7 nhp single, was built in 1908 and registered BW 4509.

161. Building a new roadway by traditional methods at a steam working provides both an attraction and an asset. This road gang in period dress and with vintage equipment to match, is at work with tar and chippings at Lightwater Valley, North Yorkshire, on the 12th September 1982. Part of D. Wood's 10 ton Fowler roller can be seen; this is No.15589, new in 1920 and registered U 8709.

162. Ploughing by steam provided one of the greatest rally attractions but demanded much space for its operation and much walking to see it! This is J.W. Desborough's 16 nhp Class BB Fowler No.15341 of 1919 working at Raynham Day rally in Norfolk on 15th September 1962. Note the 'spuds' on the rear wheel to give extra grip. RLS records suggest the roughly painted registration 'BL 8620' is incorrect; it should have been BL 8168.

163. This is a 5 furrow anti balance plough being demonstrated at Lightwater Valley, North Yorkshire, on 12th September 1981. Most ploughing was undertaken on the two-engine system with a pair of matched engines, one on each side of the field. Each engine in turn would draw the plough across the field and move forward between each pull. The plough here is being drawn by an engine to the left and at the end of its pull the second engine, to the right, will take up the strain so lowering the left hand set of shares into the soil. As the engines take up the strain at the beginning of each pull the wheel assembly is pulled forward slightly within the implement. This renders it 'out of balance' and causes the trailing plough shares to bite into the soil. The operator controls the depth of the furrows by operation of the horizontal hand wheel.

164. As well as ploughs, cultivators like giant rakes were used to break up the soil to a lesser depth. M.H. Middlewood's Fowler 9x11 tyne cultivator is working at Thirsk on 2nd October 1971. Unlike the plough, this cultivator is not reversible and is turned by the distant engine at the end of each pull. Note the location of the anchor point of the right hand engine's cable; when the next reversal has been completed the tension will rotate the 'turnabout gear' surmounting the main frame, so bringing the anchorage to the point above the front wheel as presently occupied by the left hand engine's anchorage. Other work performed by ploughing engines included harrowing and mole drainage whilst away from agriculture, lake dredging was carried out. (See photo 110.)

165. An essential activity at any rally is to keep the engines supplied with coal and water. A. Fearnley & Son's Sentinel waggon No.1465 is not only and entrant but is also taking coal to the other participants. It is at Kegworth Carnival on the 26th July 1958. The waggon was built as a 'Standard' in 1916 but was rebuilt with a 'Super' engine in 1942. It is registered AW 3321.

166. Another Sentinel Waggon, but this time an S4, is on duty at the Skegness rally on the 18th June 1960 to carry water to the other engines. Works No.8992, built in 1933 and registered TJ 4148, it is owned by G.E. Liversidge of Doncaster who had fitted the tank and a steam driven pump. The waggon was later sold and the tank removed, and it has since moved out to Australia.

167. Fairground rides first appeared at rallies as an adjunct to the engines but the older types soon acquired a prominence of their own. Then in 1964 a full scale 'Old Time Steam Fair' was held and was timed to mark the 25th anniversary of the founding of the Friendship Circle of Showland Fans. It was a three-day event from the 28th to the 30th August and took place at Shottesbrooke Park near Maidenhead, Berkshire. It proved extremely popular although there were only two steam operated rides, the yachts by Harry Lee and by Lt Com John Baldock (see photos 62 & 63). Percy Cole's Venetian Gondola ride was also present (see photos 58 & 59) but was no longer steam driven. However there were plenty of showman's road locomotives, traction engines and mechanical organs present.

ENGINE GALLERY

ENGINE MANUFACTERS

The next twenty-seven pages depict preserved engines from different manufacturers and represent the makes most likely to be seen on the rally field. Apart from concentrations in Leeds and Lincoln most traction engine builders were located away from large industrial centres, and could be found in the east and south of England where arable farming was dominant. Specialist wagon builders however were located in the north and west. The 'Sentinel' waggons were initially developed in Glasgow, otherwise there were no builders in Ireland, Scotland or Wales. One-off survivors, modern replicas, engines of freelance design, perhaps using parts from old machines, and engines built overseas may also be seen at today's rallies.

PRESERVED ENGINES

The numbers of preserved engines in the United Kingdom has been fairly static for several years. However there is now an influx of British built engines which had been exported overseas and which are now being returned for preservation. Hence the stated totals of some makers' engines may be subject to change. For a detailed record of preserved road steam vehicles in the British Isles (except for steam cars) readers are referred to The Traction Engine Register published by the Southern Counties Historic Vehicles Preservation Trust. This is continually updated with new editions.

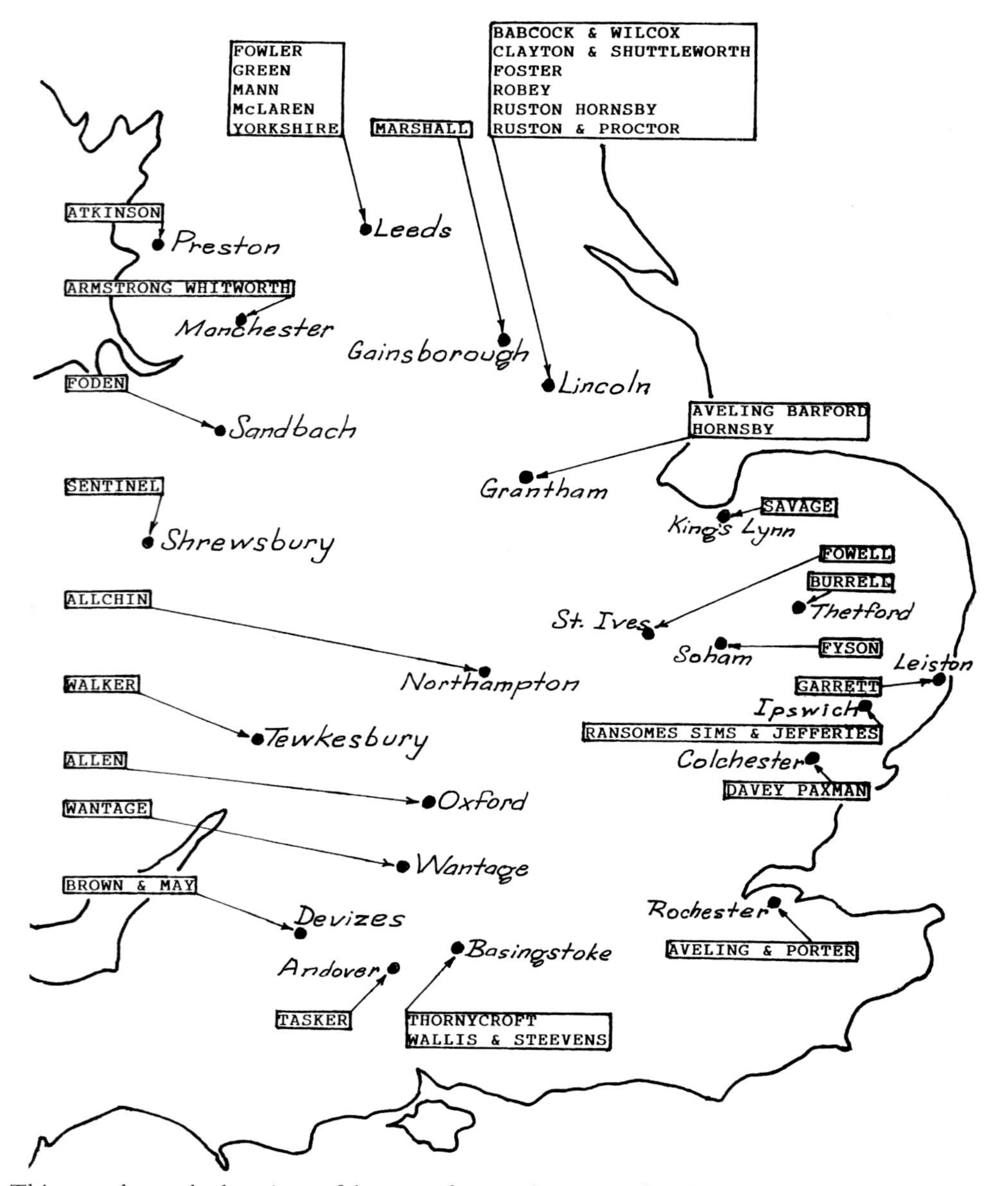

This map shows the locations of the manufacturers' premises for all the traditional British-built engines appearing in this book. Please refer to the index on page 7 for those makers not separately featured in this chapter.

168. William Allchin & Co Ltd, Globe Works, Northampton.
Allchins was a medium sized firm which built traction engines from the mid-nineteenth century together with a few road locomotives and rollers. In later years steam wagons were included in their range. This traction engine is a 7nhp single No.1105, dating from1899 when it was new to a Mr Storey of Barrowden, Rutland, and it was subsequently given local registration FP 1024. Fifty six years later, on the 23rd July 1955, it is attending the Kegworth Carnival, Leics., owned by Cyril Grice of Old Dalby, Leics., and carrying the name "ELLEN". There are about twenty Allchin engines remaining today.

169. Sir W.G. Armstrong-Whitworth Ltd, Openshaw, Manchester.
This firm included steam rollers in its production range at its Manchester factory after World War I to help alleviate a shortage in orders resulting from the run down in armaments. Over 100 rollers were produced of which seven remain. The survivors are typical three point compound rollers with piston valves although an unorthodox quick reverse tandem design with a high pitched boiler was also produced. The roller here dates from 1923, works No.10R2, and was originally owned by the Kettering UDC, Northants., where it was registered BD 7511. It is appearing at the Society's visit to the Welland Valley Vintage Traction Club at Market Harborough on the 31st May 1986 and is owned by Mick George.

170. Aveling-Barford Ltd, Invicta Works, Grantham.

The firm was formed in 1934 when Aveling & Porter Ltd joined forces with Barford & Perkins Ltd of Peterborough to set up a new company to build road making equipment and contractors plant. The new firm occupied a site which had been part of Richard Hornsby's works. Steam engine building was limited to a small range of single and compound cylinder three point rollers and some were contracted out to other builders, eg Ransomes. The example here is one of some twenty survivors and was built in 1937 for Staines UDC, works No.AC 621 and registered GMK 939. It is rated at 4 nhp, weighs 6 tons and is appearing at Kelvedon rally, Essex, on 22nd September 1962. It is owned by C. Brown of Rayne, Essex, and named "LADY HELEN".

171. Aveling & Porter Ltd, Invicta Works, Rochester, Kent.

Aveling & Porter were Britain's leading steam roller manufacturer, building a greater number than the combined total of all other manufacturers. They also built large numbers of most other types of steam road engines. In 1920 they joined the Agricultural & General Engineers combine and decline set in. However, with the AGE collapse in 1932 all was not lost as Aveling & Porter were able to amalgamate with Barford & Perkins in setting up Aveling-Barford Ltd as described on the previous page. In spite of the AGE failure there are some 600 Aveling & Porter engines remaining, a greater number than for any other manufacturer. It is inevitable that as major repairs and replacement of parts becomes necessary to keep them running, and with none of the firms featured here still in existence, it has been necessary to look elsewhere. One notable achievement has been secured for the owner of a historic Aveling traction engine brought back from Australia: a complete replacement riveted boiler has been made at Israel Newton & Sons works at Idle near Bradford. The engine above is works No.10437 and is classed as a convertible in that it can be readily changed from a traction engine to a roller and vice versa. It is owned by J.M. Edwards of Brooke, Norfolk, and is appearing at nearby Bressingham Hall on 28th August 1966. It was new to Wigtown CC and registered OS 1314, and it now is part of the Thursford Collection.

172. Brown & May Ltd, North Wilts Foundry, Devizes, Wiltshire.

The firm commenced about 1860 when Charles May withdrew from a partnership with Ransomes at Ipswich. Operations were on a small scale and although a few of their portables have survived, No.8742 above is one of only two traction engines remaining. It is a 6 nhp compound showman's 'traction engine' (sic), registered AU 4705, named "GENERAL BULLER", and is appearing during the Society's visit to the Peterborough Farm Machinery Preservation Society's open day at Thorney on the 14th May 2005. It belongs to Alan Rundle of Boston and has been in his family's ownership for many years. It was bought for thrashing so the showman's fittings were removed, but with its working days over, they have been put back. The engine was built in 1912 and was one of the last out of the works.

173. Charles Burrell & Sons Ltd, St Nicholas Works, Thetford, Norfolk.

Burrells are probably the most popular engines on the rally field and are certainly considered by some to be the best looking. Dating back to 1770, the firm commenced building traction engines in the mid-nineteenth century. Their range went on to include locomotives, showman's road locomotives, ploughing engines, rollers, tractors and wagons. Total numbers amounted to some 4000 and over 300 remain in preservation. In the depressed market following World War I Burrells joined the ill-fated Agricultural & General Engineers combine but this led to a decline in innovation and in orders. The final engine emerged from the Thetford works in 1930 and Charles Burrells was no more.

Many of their traction engines, and other types to a lesser degree, were fitted with the firm's patented single crank compound system with the cylinders arranged diagonally and the piston rods linked to a single crosshead. The system is evident in this engine, No.2003, of 6 nhp and built in 1897. It is owned by Bill Briggs of Knutsford, Cheshire, and is appearing at the Society's visit to nearby Warburton Park on the 28th April 1979 with Bill's late wife Jackie on the footplate. It carries the name "DIAMOND QUEEN" and registration YA 509.

174. Clayton & Shuttleworth Ltd, Stamp End Iron Works, Lincoln.
Nathaniel Clayton and Joseph Shuttleworth set up the firm in 1842 and it was among the earliest manufacturers of both portable and self moving engines, building both in large numbers. Rollers were later added to the range and, finally, wagons were introduced in the early twentieth century. A separate company, Clayton Wagons Ltd, was later set up to build these vehicles. The traction engine depicted is No.46823, dating from 1914, and is appearing at the Horsham Park rally, West Sussex, on 8th July 1967. It is a 7 nhp single, registered KE 4173, and was first owned by Terrys Quarries of West Malling, Kent. It was still domiciled there when the photo was taken, then in the ownership of J. Naylor and P. Fagg. It carried the plausible name "DUSTY"! No.46823 is one of some fifty Claytons remaining today.

175. Babcock & Wilcox Ltd.
Babcock & Wilcox took over Clayton & Shuttleworth in 1924 and built a number of rollers at Lincoln bearing the former name. This is one of five survivors, works No. 95/4011, a 6 ton single, built in 1926. It is appearing at the Umberleigh rally, Devon on the 6th June 1964 when owned by D. Muxworthy of nearby South Molton and named "PRIDE OF SOUTHSEA". The Babcock rollers were among the last steam engines built at the Stamp End Works.

176. Davey Paxman & Co Ltd, Standard Iron Works, Colchester.

The business commenced in the 1860s and went on to produce large numbers of portable and stationary engines but only started building traction engines in 1906. They then ceased their production in 1916, so it is hardly surprising that only five of their engines still exist. Davey Paxman joined AGE in 1919 but overcame the combine's downfall and became outstanding builders of diesel engines. Although no road steam engines were made after 1916 they did build seven 15" gauge miniature steam locomotives for the Romney Hythe & Dymchurch Railway in 1925/6. These have been particularly successful and all remain in service today.

The photo depicts 1907 build 7 nhp single traction engine No.13073, registered NK 967, owned by A.G. Evans of Wigginton, Herts., and named "DAVY CROCKETT" after a popular song of the time. It is appearing at the Appleford rally on 14th June 1958.

177. Fodens Ltd, Elworth Works, Sandbach, Cheshire.

In the 1860s Edwin Foden became a partner in the general engineering firm of Plant & Hancock, Sandbach, later taking it over and in 1887 changing the name to his own. The production range included portable, stationary and traction engines. In 1899 Fodens produced their first wagon and after much experiment created an outstanding overtype wagon with locomotive boiler and a compound engine with chain drive to the rear axle. Its success was such that in 1907 Fodens were able to concentrate on wagons to the virtual exclusion of other products. Even so they apparently wished to impress their customers with an even greater output and used only the even numbers in allocating works numbers! Production of wagons continued through the nineteen-twenties and a late attempt at a modern undertype wagon was produced, but steam production ceased in1932 when Fodens turned over to i/c engined vehicles. Perhaps the Foden feature best known to the general public was its brass band and although the firm did not build vehicles to carry passengers they made an exception for carrying their own bandsmen to performances. The vehicle concerned was works No.4364, registered M 6359, and was completed in May 1914. The 23 seat bus was named "PUFFING BILLY" and lasted until the early 1930s when it was scrapped. A replica body has been now built and placed on a later wagon, No.11340, which dates from 1923. This was originally sold to the Rock Brewery Co, Brighton, and registered CD 8223. It had several other commercial owners before being acquired by G.E. Milligan who converted it to the bus seen in the photo above and he also obtained the old Band Bus registration number which the vehicle carries today. The bus is appearing at the Great Dorset Steam Fair on 29th August 2002 where it is performing a useful service in taking visitors around the site, and is being operated by Les Searle from Horsham, West Sussex. Following 11340 is Foden No.4258 which has been adapted for passenger carrying and is operating a similar service. Some 120 Fodens still exist, a few are traction engines or road locomotives, but most are the familiar overtype wagons or tractors.

178. William Foster & Co Ltd, Wellington Foundry, Lincoln.

Fosters established their works in Lincoln in 1899 although the firm's origin dates back to 1856. They manufactured a variety of stationary and portable engines and, in later years, traction engines, tractors and road locomotives, including a series of showman's engines in the 1920s and 1930s. In 1909, in cooperation with Richard Hornsby, they produced a steam tracked vehicle and undertook the design of tanks during World War I. Henceforth their builders plates incorporated the tank motif shown in the inset. Some fifty Foster engines survive and this engine is No.14589, a 4 nhp 5 ton compound tractor, built in 1927 and registered UT 2109. It is appearing at the East Anglian Traction Engine Club's rally at Saling, Essex, on the 9th July 1955 having been entered by Harold Darby of Ely and is named "LORD OF THE ISLES".

179. C.J. Fowell & Co Ltd, Cromwell Engineering Works, St. Ives, Hunts.
The firm was set up by George Fowell in 1876 after he had been working for Burrells. Engine production was limited; just 109 traction engines were built and mostly to a generally similar design. Seven survive and this one, No.98, was built in 1909 and registered CE 7858. First delivered to F.J. Hunt of nearby Guilden Morden, it continued in commercial use at Redbourn, Herts., and at Horsham, West Sussex. Moving on to the preservation era it is seen at the Penshurst rally, Kent, on the 20th August 1960, in the ownership of W. Chandler of Smallfield, Surrey.

180. John Fowler & Co (Leeds) Ltd, Steam Plough Works, Leeds.

John Fowler was born in 1826 and was pre-eminent in the development of ploughing by steam. In his early days, engines and tackle were built by others but in 1862 he had set up his own business in Leeds which went from strength to strength despite the founder's tragic and early death in 1864. As the works expanded, not only ploughing engines but all other types of engine were produced and some 500 survive today, a total only exceeded by Aveling & Porter. Fowler ploughing engines are seen at work in photos 105, 106 and others, but featured here is a typical Fowler compound traction engine and, like Fowell on the previous page, it is appearing at the Penshurst rally on 20th August 1960. It is works No.9924, built in 1904, registered BP 5767, and had various commercial owners in West Sussex. It is in the ownership of Robert Whitehead of Tonbridge and is being driven by professional engineman Bill Newell.

181. Richard Garrett & Sons Ltd, Leiston, Suffolk.

The beginnings of the firm date from1778 when Richard Garrett set up a tool making business in Leiston. Output gradually expanded with their first portable and stationary engines appearing in the 1840s and the first road engine in 1857. Henceforth production ranged over most forms of engine and much else besides but their greatest achievement was probably their number 4 CD tractor, introduced in 1906 (see photos 112, 153, & 157). Garretts joined the AGE combine in 1920 and after the latter's collapse, the Manchester locomotive builders, Beyer Peacock & Co Ltd, gained a controlling interest and henceforth Garretts participated in producing parts for railway locomotives. An unusual feature for a road locomotive manufacturer; Garretts had their own private siding and employed their own steam shunting locomotive (see photo 100).

Something approaching one hundred Garrett engines survive, the majority being tractors, but there is also a sprinkling of traction engines, rollers and wagons. Rarer still are their road locomotives and this is works No. 27946, a 6 nhp 16 ton engine, built in 1909 and carrying Belfast registration OI 6818. It had been built for John Harkness & Co and worked in the Belfast shipyards. In retirement it is seen at Lightwater Valley, North Yorkshire, on the 12th September 1981 in the ownership of P.C.W. Rhodes and carries the name "VERA".

182. Thomas Green & Son Ltd, Smithfield Ironworks, Leeds.

Greens initially set up a works in Hunslet but moved to larger premises north of the City Centre, taking over a handsome hotel in the process which served as their offices. Their production was not large but they secured niche markets in road rollers as well as steam trams and grass cutters. Five steam rollers survive, this one is 8 ton machine No.1968 which had been built in 1917 for the War Department. It subsequently joined the Devon County Council fleet and, still in their ownership, is appearing at the Umberleigh rally on 6th June 1964. It carries Devon CC registration TA 2431.

The inset shows a Leeds Civic Trust blue plaque which has been mounted on the office block, having been unveiled in 2001. Similar plaques have been provided at the sites of other Leeds engine builders.

183. Mann's Patent Steam Cart & Wagon Co Ltd, Pepper Road Works, Leeds.
Leeds manufacturer Mann & Charlesworth Ltd produced conventional traction engines at their Canning Works during the 1890s, many incorporating J.H. Mann's patent single eccentric reversing gear. In 1899 the partnership was dissolved and Mann's Patent Steam Cart & Wagon Co was set up with premises at Pepper Road on the outskirts of Hunslet. The new firm concentrated on unusual designs of light wagons and tractors which were both operated and fired from the side of the boiler to avoid interference with the payload area. Light rollers were also produced which, with quick reversal provided by the patent gear, made them ideal for patching work. A dozen Mann's vehicles have survived but just one of them is a roller and it is seen at the Elham rally in Kent on the 30th July 1955 when owned by David Barlow. It dates from 1919 with works No. 1145 and registration KM 514.

184. Marshall, Sons & Co Ltd, Britannia Ironworks, Gainsborough.

Marshalls were a long established Lincolnshire manufacturer and built their first traction engine in the 1870s. They went on to become one of Britain's leading producers and also built tractors and rollers as well as an extensive range of portable and stationary engines. Two typical single cylinder general purpose engines are seen here, both are rated at 6 nhp and they are at the Harewood rally on the 1st September 1969. On the left is F.J. & P. Harrison's "BLACK BESS", new in 1900, works No.32092 and registered PY 5827 whilst to its right is A.C. Rockliff's "SURPRISE", new in 1934, works No.87003 and registered TL 3612. These are two of some 350 survivors from the Britannia Ironworks, the third largest total from a British manufacturer.

185. J. & H. McLaren Ltd, Midland Engine Works, Leeds.

The firm was founded in 1876 when brothers John and Henry McLaren set up their plant in Jack Lane, Hunslet. They produced road engines of various types and were also notable builders of large stationary engines for electricity generation. In the nineteen-twenties steam engine production ceased and they developed a very successful range of diesel engines in association with the German manufacturer Benz. Over thirty steam road engines survive of which twenty are traction engines. This one is No.1038, built in 1909, of 8 nhp and registered CT 4212. In the ownership of Graham Whitwell of York, it is appearing at the Harrogate rally on 10th June 2000.

186. Ransomes, Sims & Jefferies Ltd, Orwell Works, Ipswich.
Robert Ransome moved his metal working business from Norwich to Ipswich in the late eighteenth century. Henceforth, operating from a number of sites in the town and under a number of titles, the firm expanded to becomes a major builder of stationary, portable and traction engines, and built the country's first practical self-moving road engine in the late eighteen-forties. Tractors and wagons were later added to the range and one of their greatest achievements was the series of road steam vehicles for the Indian Government around 1870 to the designs of R.W. Thomson. Unfortunately no Thomson road steamer by any maker has survived but nearly 100 other Ransomes engines remain in preservation, approximately half being traction engines. The example here is a 7 nhp single, works No.26995 and registered EW 2320. It is owned by R.E. Gale of Whittlesey near Peterborough and is taking its turn in the parade at the Skegness rally on the 18th June 1960.

187. Robey & Co Ltd, Globe Works, Lincoln.
Robert Robey founded the company in 1854 and it grew to become one of the country's larger manufacturers embracing many types of road engine including traction engines, tractors, rollers and wagons as well as portable and stationary engines. A distinguished later design was a quick reverse tandem roller (see photo 28) but the traction engine here is rather older and dates from 1910. It is appearing at the 'Expo '77' on the Peterborough Showground on the 29th August 1977 and is an overhead valve compound, works No.29330, and carries Kesteven registration CT 4101. It was originally supplied to F.B. Gibbons & Sons Ltd of Market Deeping.
Some thirty Robey engines remain, a third of them being tandem rollers, some of which have been modified to tri-tandem.

188. Ruston, Proctor & Co Ltd, Sheaf Ironworks, Lincoln.

In 1840 Proctor & Burton set up at Lincoln as millwrights and engineers and they were joined in 1857 by Joseph Ruston. Mr Burton withdrew in the same year and the title above was then created, although incorporation did not occur until 1899. Portable engines soon appeared and the first traction engine was built in 1876. The firm expanded into many branches of engineering, particularly with oil and gas engines, and exported to many countries but when World War I contracts were coming to an end their directors realised that with the inevitable loss of overseas markets they would face difficulties. It was then that they were approached by another Lincolnshire firm facing similar problems; Richard Hornsby & Sons Ltd. As a result the latter went into voluntary liquidation, their assets being acquired by Ruston, Proctor and the new firm, Ruston & Hornsby Ltd, was set up in 1918. This became a powerful and successful company and is outlined on page 164.

The handsome roller portrayed above is Ruston, Proctor No.48359, an 11 ton Class SCR compound built in 1913 and registered TA 2894. It was delivered new to James Murch & Sons Ltd of Little Torrington, Devon, and is appearing at the neighbouring Umberleigh rally on the 6th June 1964. It carries the name "PRIDE OF BARUM" and has a chimney purported to have come from one of the Lynton & Barnstaple Railway's Manning Wardle locomotives. The roller is one of some twenty engines remaining from before the 1918 merger.

189. Richard Hornsby & Sons Ltd, Spittlegate Ironworks, Grantham.
Richard Hornsby and a Mr Seaman established a foundry in Grantham in 1815. The latter retired in 1828 and the business then remained with the Hornsby family until it became a limited liability company in 1880. This in turn continued until it joined with Ruston, Proctor in 1918. Engine manufacture commenced with portables in 1849 and their first traction engine was built in 1863. Stationary engines were also built. However in 1891 Hornsbys started building oil engines to the designs of Herbert Ackroyd Stuart and steam engine production declined. From 1906 only oil engines were built. The illustration is of Richard Hornsby No.6557, an 8 nhp single traction engine built in 1887 and registered FL 2598. It was delivered new to Ratcliffe & Co of Derby but spent most of its working life with Gibbons & Son of Castor near Peterborough. Now named "MAGGIE" it is appearing at the Great Dorset Steam Fair on the 3rd September 2004. It is one of only three Hornsby traction engines remaining in Britain although, as with many other builders, several portables have also survived.

190. Ruston & Hornsby Ltd, Sheaf Ironworks, Lincoln.
With the wide ranging scope of the business at its formation in 1918, the role of steam engine production was of limited importance. Nevertheless the Ruston, Proctor series of traction engines, rollers and tractors was maintained together with many sizes of portable engines. Numbers tailed off in the late nineteen-twenties and the last steam engine was built in 1936. Some twenty-five road engines have survived together with a dozen or so portables. The engine here is 5 nhp traction engine No.169166 built in 1933 and registered TL 3433. Named "QUEEN BESS" and in the ownership of the Crowther family of Skipton, it is appearing at the Pickering rally on the 10th August 1963.

191. The Sentinel Waggon Works Ltd, Sentinel Works, Shrewsbury.

In 1906 the Glasgow engineering firm of Alley & McLellan produced an undertype steam waggon incorporating a vertical boiler and a duplex horizontal engine under the floor with chain drive to the rear axle. This was a time of experiment, with many firms taking part in building steam wagons, and whilst many fell by the wayside, the 'Sentinel' waggon as it was known (with two 'g's) continued to prosper. Space for the addition of large scale waggon production at the Glasgow site was limited and so a separate company was set up in new premises at Shrewsbury, opening in 1915-17. The production line for these early waggons, the 'Standard' as it became known, was maintained until 1923 when the 'Super' was introduced (photo 72). This was in turn superseded by the double geared 'DG' models in 1927 (photo 71) and finally the revolutionary 'S' type was introduced in 1933 (photo 68). Total production of the four types amounted to over 6500 waggons and in addition several special vehicles were produced (eg see photo 95). Some 120 Sentinel steam road vehicles remain in Britain today. Sentinels also built hundreds of steam railway vehicles, notably shunting locomotives and passenger railcars.

Brown Bayley Steels has already been mentioned (see photo 77) and the photo above is No. 6 of their fleet of 'Standards' after its restoration. It is works No.1286, built in 1916 and registered in Salop AW 2964. It is appearing at the Pickering rally on the 10th August 1969 but it has since been moved to the Glasgow Transport Museum, a fitting venue as although assembled in Shrewsbury, the waggon's design has a close affinity with its Glaswegian parentage.

192. William Tasker & Sons Ltd, Waterloo Ironworks, Andover, Hampshire.

Taskers built their first traction engine in 1869 and production of road steam vehicles continued until 1928. Rollers and wagons were produced later in the period but their most successful designs were the 'Little Giant' tractors (see photo 116). In the post-steam period they concentrated on trailers including during World War II the famous 'Queen Mary' design for carrying aircraft. In their closing years the management built up a superb museum collection of Tasker tools patterns, implements and of course engines but then financial failure of the firm led to the contents being put up for auction in 1969. Luckily many of the lots , including several engines, were secured by the Tasker Trust set up by Hampshire County Council and these have since been housed in Winchester, and examples can be seen at Basingstoke's Milestones Museum (see photo 207).

Nearly half of the thirty four surviving Tasker engines are in the County Council collection but the 5 nhp compound traction engine above is not one of them. It is works No.1709, built in 1916 and registered PU 4724, and is appearing at the Saffron Walden Steam Festival on the 15th June 1957.

193. Wallis & Steevens Ltd, North Hants Ironworks, Basingstoke, Hampshire.

Arthur Wallis opened his agricultural engineering business in 1856, in partnership with James Haslam. Charles Steevens soon joined them but after two or three years Haslam retired. The firm had been building portables from around 1860 and they introduced their first design of traction engine in 1877. One feature unique to some Wallis & Steevens traction engines was the use of an automatic expansion gear whereby cut off is controlled by the governor and not a throttle valve in the steam supply as is usually the case. This was first applied to No. 2303 in May 1895. The principle of using the expansive properties of steam was well understood and had been applied to stationary engines by a number of engine builders but Wallis and Steevens were able to patent the application to traction engines and were alone in using the system. The firm produced a very wide range of steam engines from tiny vertical stationary engines, to moderately sized fixed horizontal engines, portables, road locomotives, tractors and wagons but there is no doubt that the firm's forte was rollers. From the first single cylindered roller in 1891 a steady trade of reliable machines was built up, some with expansion gear and some compounds, and then in 1923 came the revolutionary 'Advance' design, (see photos 31 & 32). Several hundred of these were built in 6, 8 & 10 ton sizes, the last steamer in 1940, but by that time the design had been successfully adapted for oil engine propulsion. Another innovation, hard on the heels of the 'Advance', was the 'Simplicity' (see photo 34). Very few were built as it seemed that there was little demand for such small steam rollers. Nearly 80 'Advance' but just six 'Simplicity' rollers remain out of some 180 preserved Wallis engines.

The subject above is obviously not a roller. It is an early light weight single cylinder tractor appearing at the first Andover rally on 6th April 1953 and is being driven by its then owner, Giles Romanes, whose earlier exploits at Nettlebed and Appleford are seen in photos 129 & 130. The engine is named "GOLIATH" and it carries a then recently issued Berkshire CC registration GRX 400. This is because its builder's plate is missing and its antecedents cannot be confirmed. Most likely it was No. 2694, originally sold to Pickfords in 1904. Giles Romanes still owns "GOLIATH" and he has regularly taken it to the Great Dorset Steam Fair right up to the 40th anniversary event in 2008.

194. Wantage Engineering Co Ltd, Wantage, Berkshire.

A foundry was in existence at Wantage in the eighteen-twenties serving the needs of local farmers and became known as the Vale of White Horse Foundry. This developed under a succession of owners and in 1887, with Gibbons and Robinson in command, the first traction engine was produced. Control of the firm soon passed to Robinson & Auden Ltd but with the continuing agricultural depression, financial difficulties were experienced. To maintain both production and local employment, the local MP, Sir Robert J. Loyd-Lindsay, VC, came to the rescue taking over the assets and setting up the Wantage Engineering Co Ltd in 1900. He made a heavy investment and the firm then carried on successfully for many years, although Sir Robert died just after its formation. The product range included portable and traction engines, and an undertype tractor was also produced. Their last traction engine came out in 1913.

Just two traction engines survive from the later regime (one appears in photos 144 & 145) whilst the traction engine above is the sole survivor of the Robinson & Auden partnership. An older traction engine from the Gibbons and Robinson era and a few portable engines from various periods still exist with one dating back to the 1870s when brothers P. & H.P. Gibbons were running the business. The engine depicted above is 6 nhp single No. 1376 dating from 1900 and registered AD 8889. It is driving a saw bench at the Lightwater Valley steam working in North Yorkshire on the 12th September 1981.

195. The Yorkshire Patent Steam Wagon Co Ltd, Hunslet, Leeds.

An unusual design of 'double return flue boiler' was patented in 1901 which fitted transversely across the frames at the front of a wagon. The firebox was in the centre and the combustion gases then separated, going to one end of the boiler or the other, and then returning through other sets of tubes to discharge to the central chimney. The patentee was G.H. Mann, brother of J.H. Mann of the Mann's Patent Steam Cart & Wagon Co. However the latter showed little interest in the design so a separate concern, title as above, was set up in 1902, the two works having adjacent premises in Pepper Road, Hunslet. The distinctive 'Yorkshire' wagon, incorporating the patented boiler, soon developed into a viable product and output was maintained well into the early nineteen-thirties. A cardan shaft drive version was produced but most wagons had chain drive to the rear axle from a vertical compound engine behind or alongside the driver, who in turn sat behind the boiler. The illustration shows works No.940, built in 1917, attending the Harewood rally on 31st August 1970. It had spent its working life in Leeds and ended up in a scrap yard at Hunslet Moor. It was then rescued by Tom Varley who made an excellent job of its restoration and named it "PENDLE QUEEN". It carries Leeds registration U 4245. Only six Yorkshire wagons still survive in the UK.

PRESERVATION COMES OF AGE

196. Preserved steam vehicles are not confined to rallies and they can add interest to many a public event. Two examples appear on this page, both in the City of York, with on the right, Father Christmas being taken from York Station to his grotto in the local Cooperative department store. The engine, Foster No.14632 "SUCCESS", has appeared before, in photo 156, but now owned by L.C. Byass & Son of Little Weighton near Hull, it is undertaking this pleasurable task on the 6th November 1971.

197 In St Helen's Square in the centre of the City, another showman's road locomotive appears to be involved in a rather melancholy event. But it is not all it seems as the coffin only contains signatures. These are destined for the Lord Mayor and are petitioning for a projected national railway museum to be set up in York rather than in London. I do not need to tell readers that the petitioners' aspirations were fulfilled. The engine is Monty Thackray's "EVENING STAR", Fowler No.14862 of 1917 and registered DW 2235. The date is 20th October 1970.

198. Engines were exported from Britain to many countries and inevitably there are survivors overseas of types extinct in this country – and there are enthusiasts here eager to get hold of them. A good example is this Atkinson wagon brought back from Australia in 1976 by Tom Varley, who then restored it and gave it this elaborate livery. Atkinsons & Co Ltd of Preston built steam wagons during and after World War I before abandoning steam in favour of internal combustion designs: this is believed to be works No.72 built in 1918. It has been accorded Preston registration CK 209. It is in steam at Tom Varley's caravan park at Gisburn, Lancs., during a Society visit on the 14th May 1977. It is the only Atkinson steam wagon surviving in the U.K.

199. A more recent repatriation is this Fowler Class B6 road locomotive built in 1911. It is works No.12906 which had been supplied new to Charles Openshaw of Reading and is presumed to have been requisitioned by the War Department for use in France during World War I. The engine stayed there after the war and its continued survival in the southwest of the country near Toulouse has been known for many years. It apparently remains in reasonable condition although its smokebox and chimney are among items needing replacement. It has now been purchased by Richard Willcox, Chairman of the Road Locomotive Society, and brought back to England. The photo shows it at Chippenham, Wiltshire, in April 2008 and it is hoped it will not be too long before it is restored to working order. (RICHARD WILLCOX)

200. It was inevitable that as the numbers of preserved engines grew so did the tendency for owners to modify them to suit their wishes, much to the annoyance of those who thought that they should be preserved in their commercial guise. However with large numbers of rollers surviving, and with their limited capabilities on the rally field, they are candidates for conversion, and the November 2002 Road Locomotive Society Journal listed 115 rollers that had been turned into traction engines or tractors. This roller was one of them, Aveling & Porter No. 14068, built in 1930 and registered VN 2092. Prior to conversion it is appearing at North Yorkshire's Stillington rally on the 28th June 1970 and is owned by Robert Oliver of Bishop Auckland.

201. Two years later the same roller has been converted to a showman's type tractor and fitted with large pneumatic tyres. The photo was taken on the 18th November 1972 at an Edwardian and Modern Steam Fair held at York's Fulford Barracks.

202. Another but rarer tendency is to marry different chassis and engine parts to produce some unusual vehicles. This bus is a toast rack seated vehicle, one of a fleet of four which operated a sea front service at Skegness from 1926 until 1958. Following withdrawal it was acquired by David Potter of Yaxham, Norfolk, who removed its petrol engine and some of the seats and mounted an Aveling & Porter boiler and engine in the middle of the body. In this guise it is attending a rally at Raynham, Norfolk, on the 15th September 1962. It is thought the boiler came from Aveling & Porter No. 9095, an East Suffolk County Council roller dating from 1920.

203. Yet another strange combination is this Morris Cowley chassis converted to steam operation. It is at the Kegworth Carnival on the 23rd July 1955 but I have no further details.

204. Passenger carrying vehicles have already been mentioned, see photo 177, but no steam bus has seen public service on a highway in Britain sine the nineteen-twenties. This has now changed and Vernon Smith and Viv Hamilton have been operating regular tours around the streets of Whitby in the holiday season since 2006. A new rather stylish body has been mounted on Sentinel DG6 No. 8590, which was built in 1931 as an open waggon and registered GT 2827. It is seen with passengers aboard in the centre of Whitby on 23rd August 2007.

205. With some 3000 preserved road steam vehicles in Britain there would seem to be little desire to build more but both replicas and new designs are increasingly being produced, albeit in small numbers. This example comes under the 'new design' category and is appearing at the Bedfordshire Steam & Country Fayre on the 16th September 2007. Entered by J. & P. Kilgour it is described in the programme as a *'Spider Prototype Mk 2 Steam Lorry – a general purpose on and off road 4WD machine built by the owner. Chain drive is taken from a two cylinder double acting high pressure engine to a 4-speed gearbox. It is capable of 25mph.'*

206. To most television viewers, 'engines' will conjure up just one name – Fred Dibnah. The steeplejack from Bolton first became famous for scaling mill chimneys and perhaps more so for their demolition. With his natural ability for giving clear explanations for all things mechanical and architectural, he widened the scope of his programmes and so the British public were introduced to his two beloved engines, both by Aveling & Porter, a steam roller and a convertible traction engine. The latter, seen here, is No. 7838, built in 1912 for West Sussex County Council but later serving with Devon CC where it was registered TA 2436. Fred was awarded an MBE for services to television and the day of the ceremony, the 7th July 2004, found him parked in London's Wellington Barracks, just a stone's throw from Buckingham Palace. On the following day, with the ordeal over, Fred went sightseeing and, with his son Jack steering, he is heading along Great George Street towards Parliament Square. Sadly Fred did not have long to celebrate his achievement as he died on the 6th November in the same year.

(KEITH LANGSTON)

207. The early concept that engines would only survive in museums has fortunately not come about. Even so there are several engines appearing as 'show case' exhibits in museums (see photo 121) but there are now several more entertaining museums, both private and publicly owned, that place engines in appropriate settings. Perhaps the finest is the Hampshire County Council's Milestones Museum at Basingstoke where, with three engine builders once based in the area (Tasker, Thornycroft and Wallis & Steevens), a dozen local engines appear. Seen here is Wallis & Steevens No. 2149, a 6 nhp convertible traction engine built in 1890 and registered BP 9469. Number 2149 was the first of its type produced by the firm and spent all its working life in West Sussex, mostly with Carter Brothers of Billingshurst. It is owned and was restored by Gerald Whitaker of Liphook and is on display in the museum when not being rallied by its owner and family. The photograph was taken on the 4th October 2001.

208. Not only have the builders of the engines portrayed in these pages vanished but most of their premises have gone too. It is therefore pleasing that the Long Shop Museum has been established in part of the former Garrett works at Leiston, Suffolk, and this forms the backdrop to this photo. The engine is an appropriate Garrett product, tractor No.33295 of 1918, registered NH 5567, named "PRINCESS ROYAL" and belonging to Charles Saunders of Huntingdon. The occasion is a Road Locomotive Society visit on the 16th May 1992 and, with two founder members, Alan Duke (left) and John Stone, this gives a fitting conclusion to this review of 'The Transitional Years'. It is no exaggeration to say that without Alan Duke's devotion to compiling engine details and licensing authorities lists over most of his lifetime, a lot of the information given in this book would not have been recorded and much of it would have been lost for all time.